THE SMALL BUSINESS

OWNERS HANDBOOK

Created by Sharon Brown

MO2VATE MEDIA

Published by The Book Chief Publishing House 2022
Suite 2A, Blackthorn House, St Paul's Square, Birmingham, B3 1RL
www.thebookchief.com

Book Cover Design: Deearo Marketing
Editor: Laura Billingham
Typesetting / Formatting / Publishing: Sharon Brown

THE BOOK CHIEF®

IGNITE YOUR WRITING

Table of Contents

FOREWORD

By Phil Horrod
WorkLife180 Coaching

When I studied to be a Chartered Management Accountant early on in my career, I had to read numerous business books and have continued to do so ever since qualifying many years ago.

However, I've never been fortunate enough to have read a business book as practical as The Small Business Owners Handbook, nor one that covers such a wide range of essential topics for small business owners, to help them successfully run their businesses.

I met Sharon Brown online several years ago and was absolutely amazed at the variety of her own business activities, including running a monthly magazine, helping authors write and publish their books and promoting and supporting public speakers. All aimed at making business owners more credible and visible in a very crowded world.

I have personally benefitted from working with Sharon and Mo2vate Media, through each area of her business services. This has included contributing to three separate books, writing several magazine articles and being promoted to speaker event co-ordinators across the UK.

I would thoroughly recommend all small business owners to take a look at doing the same, after reading this Handbook.

If you're an entrepreneurial small business owner, or looking to become one, you'll gain hugely valuable insights from reading The Small Business Owners Handbook and then keeping it afterwards, to refer to when needed.

Written by 20 subject matter experts, like me, you'll not find another business book like it anywhere else.

INTRODUCTION

Thank you for purchasing a copy of this book.

All Authors who have contributed to this book are also contributing article writers for MO2VATE Magazine (Media). The wealth of knowledge they share as a collective group would always warrant a fantastic book such as this.

For small business owners, this is business gold as they will learn the basic understanding of many covered areas that all business owners need to deal with at one point or another.

The writers shared their experiences but made it very simple for the reader to implement and realise certain aspects.

The aim of putting this book together is to share knowledge across industries and allow the reader to understand that every business owner can and will go through the same challenges at any given point in their career.

All business owners are invited to submit an article to MO2VATE Media (we're changing our name from MO2VATE Magazine). In doing so, they will be allowed to take part in these 'article' books if their article is published and subsequent speaking events related to these books.

ANNA GOODWIN

**BUSINESS OWNER AT
ANNA GOODWIN
ACCOUNTANCY LTD**

CHAPTER 1

Five Ways to Impactful Planning

By Anna Goodwin

In this period of uncertainty, do you find that business planning seems to be the last thing on your mind?

You're possibly firefighting daily and worrying about how you'll survive the next week, let alone the next twelve months! However, it's exactly when the future is unclear that taking some time out to prepare is essential.

Not only does it give a better focus and direction for your business, but it also puts you in the best place when things become a bit more settled.

If you're honest, you would probably admit that planning is often one of those tasks on your list that feels overwhelming and so never gets done.

But the benefits of creating a business plan far outweigh the effort. Trust me on this!

Here are five steps to help you plan with impact:

Make sure everything is as organised as possible. Is all of your filing up to date and has everything been entered on to your accounting system? (Or it could be a set of spreadsheets, as long as you keep them up to date). Do you know the year-end of your business? If not, you can find out by looking at Companies House (for limited companies). If you're a sole trader, the easiest way is to look at previous tax returns. The start date provides you with a date from which to begin in your accounts and a timescale for your plan. If you don't have a separate business bank account, I would recommend getting one.

Set your business goals. These are essential for a successful plan. Don't be afraid to think big.

Now is your time to state what you want to accomplish. The goals can then be broken down into actions. Think about where your business is now and which direction you want to take it. perhaps you want to increase your income by 20% in the next year? What do you need to put in place now to achieve those goals?

Give yourself some time away from your business to let your mind wander and ideas come to you. Ask yourself – is your structure the most tax efficient? Are you happy with your accounting system? Will you need to register for VAT? Have you considered your exit plan?

Once you have your plan based on your business goals, you can prepare a budget. This can be for any period you choose, but I would recommend a year starting from the first day of your accounting period. Enter all your income and expenditure from your accounting system into the budget.

The key to success is to keep it up to date by reviewing it regularly and make any necessary amendments. Remember this is a working document!

Devote some time to organising, planning and setting a budget for your business, and don't forget to celebrate those successes as you achieve your goals – no matter how small. You deserve it!

ELLIE LACROSSE

BUSINESS OWNER AT
MAISON FRAIS LTD
GLADDEN HOMES LTD

CHAPTER 2

How to BOSS Your Podcast

By Ellie LaCrosse

Want to podcast but have no idea how to start?

I admit that I stumbled into podcasting about three years ago when encouraged to sign up for an expensive studio package from a business contact. I was understandably nervous and grateful for the technical handholding from the studio, and quickly found I enjoyed it as I'm a natural talker.

I gained enough confidence to investigate and research how podcasting could leverage my brand messages and vision to a wider audience.

If you are thinking of starting a podcast

Firstly, understand why you want to broadcast your podcast in the first place and how to do it.

Research your 'why'. Ask yourself, do you enjoy chatting to people, and crucially, if your voice is clear? It is not about accents, more the clarity of your voice.

Podcasting should be seen as a tool in your marketing plan, driving traffic to your website, raising your social media profile, and positioning yourself as a collaborator with others in your industry.

Podcasting is a very niched broadcast that is used to inform, educate, or entertain a target audience. The tone of the broadcast will depend on who you want to attract as listeners.

The appeal and explosive growth is due to the ease with which the recording technologies have become more accessible.

You don't have to have to be a sound engineer to become a podcast host. There are various podcast platforms such as Spotify or Apply that provide free tutorials and various self-teaching books to help if you don't want to use a studio package.

Do you want to do studio recording or use a podcast app on your phone?
I now love doing my own podcasts from, my smartphone! I decided to install the Anchor.Fm App on my phone. I have learnt by trial and error to edit recordings and invite several guests to participate in a live recording.

The App sorts out the distribution to the major platforms at the touch of a button. You can start just using an App on your phone. That is the allure, you can act quickly, progress your skill level and upgrade as you become more confident. I'm at the stage of upgrading my recording space and adding new bits of kit to produce a better sound quality for my growing number of listeners.

Some tips for fledgling podcast hosts

One tip is to muffle extraneous sounds by covering the hard surface of the space around you with curtains or a blanket. Secondly, if inviting guest speakers, always let them know the format and have a quick run through. It keeps nerves at bay. I find scripting a basic introduction and having a couple of icebreaking questions for guests to get conversation flowing sounds more professional.

I am now learning how to monetise my podcast channel, which is on my 'to do list' for later this year.

HELEN PINKETT

BUSINESS OWNER AT
BE WELL
HELEN PINKETT BUSINESS
SUPPORT

CHAPTER 3

Overcoming Imposter Syndrome

By Helen Pinkett

Do you ever fear being uncovered as a fraud?

Doubt your abilities?

Feel like you don't deserve success?

You are not alone…

Imposter Syndrome is common in both sexes (although more prevalent in women). Sheryl Sandberg, CEO of Facebook, talks of it in her book; Lady Gaga says she has to pinch herself to remind herself of how far she has come; Tom Hanks, Maya Angelou, Arianna Huffington and many other celebrities have spoken out about suffering with this issue.

It can literally stop you in your tracks, keep you playing small and stop you enjoying your well-earned success. With feelings of inadequacy and self-doubt, you fear being uncovered and revealed as a fraud which can make you anxious and unable to push forward with confidence and ease.

Imposter Syndrome or fraud complex as it's sometimes known, is uncomfortable and is stopping so many people from fully embracing their success. It's a self-sabotaging behaviour which boils down to self-worth. The good news is that it can be overcome. Here are my top tips:

Acknowledge:

When the imposter feeling creeps in it's important to take a look at what's going on and put things into perspective. Journaling can help to work through things. Note down the situation and how you are feeling, get it all out and down onto paper. Reading back through it can help to understand the triggers and what's going on.

Talk:

You will not be the only one in your circle or business network feeling this way. Reach out to trusted friends and talk about how you are feeling. Chatting about what's going on and being honest can start a conversation where you can be open with your fears.

Understand:

Know yourself well. By being aware of what your strengths and weaknesses are, it helps you to be more confident in your abilities.

Own it:

Celebrate your successes, be proud of what you have achieved. By focusing on what's gone well you are opening up to the positives and boosting your confidence. I recommend having a notebook dedicated to your daily wins; it's great to read when imposter syndrome strikes.

Love:

Boost your self-worth by treating yourself with more kindness and compassion, lose the perfectionism and enjoy your accomplishments.

Imposter Syndrome affects people in all walks of life; some of the most confident people you meet might be struggling with it on some level so it's worth remembering that we are all trying to figure it out.

IAN
LLEWELLYN-NASH

BUSINESS OWNER AT
TONUVA COACHING

CHAPTER 4

Leading with Emotional Intelligence

By Ian Llewellyn-Nash

Emotional Intelligence has a significant foothold in personal, professional, and organisational ways of thinking and ways of working. Arguably it still attracts attention as a tool for recruitment and retention strategies and for progressive organisations to address issues around employee engagement and productivity.

Possibly, a key question remains even today, despite some 40 years of publications about the concept; "why is it important to be emotionally intelligent?"

Is technical competence enough? By that, I allude to sector-related effective decision-making, knowledge, skills, and experience relevant to the role.

Is that enough? Granted, that really doesn't matter how many group hugs a leader may give his / her team if they can't do their job.

Yet, growing emotional intelligence research in the leadership field is demonstrating that the effective awareness and management of emotions within the work setting by leaders (of their own and others emotions) enhances performance, productivity, employee engagement, and the financial scorecard.

Emotional Intelligence, since it was brought out of the cloistered halls of academic research by Goleman in his book "Emotional Intelligence" (1995) has been a concept linked to claims about leadership advantage and subsequent workplace effectiveness, decision making and ultimately profitability.

If an organisation stands still, it is unlikely to grow. Change in any organisational setting tends to be synonymous with conflict. These episodes are inherently emotion laden. Doubtless, a range of emotions will be experiences by some, if not all; excitement, enthusiasm, anxiety, anger. Both sets will have a direct impact on performance and output (whatever that means in your context).

Leaders who have Emotional Intelligence awareness can, it would seem, improve the emotional climate of their organisations, and thus enhance job performance and productivity.

The higher an individual's level of emotional intelligence the more enables is an individual to adapt to change processes by being open to new ideas, learning and levels of receptivity.

Emotional Intelligence is important in the levels of achievement by leaders, managers, executives as it offers a basis for building positive relationships, trust, understanding and openness to adjustments.

When you consider that change, and conflict is intimately associated with the day to day operational lifeworld of complex organisations – whichever sector – alongside a set of technical competencies, emotional intelligence is vital in ongoing organisational performance.

Emotional Intelligence development is predicated on behavioural change and a longitudinal approach. Raising awareness is one thing (classroom), embodying is another (coaching). Positive role models play an important part here.

Applying effective emotionally intelligent coaching programmes to individuals already within an organisation can be both cost effective and added value to the organisation.

Action/Thinking Points:

Activity 1:

Think of a good leader / manager / co-worker whom you have encountered in your work context. What words and / or phrases capture what was good about them?

Activity 2:

Choose three feelings from the list below that you want to encourage in your team.

Absorbed / Capable / Challenged / Confident / Curious / Empowered / Encouraged / Energised / Engaged / Enthusiastic / Inspired / Interested / Intrigued / Motivated / Optimistic / Receptive / Resourceful / Safe / Stimulated / Understood / Valued.

What can you do this week to build space for a more emotionally intelligent way of working, relating, leading?

CHAPTER 5

Strategic Anticipation

By Ian Llewellyn-Nash

In the light of COVID-19, businesses have had to change the way their services are offered. With that has come a new set of working challenges.

Often as agents of change in the services we offer, we overlook the need to manage change in our own business offering. I often tell my nursing students that one of our greatest strengths is routine. We know what we are doing each day, and it helps with planning service delivery. Workforce planning etc. Yet, routine is also our greatest weakness because it can lead to being reactive in nature and not proactive or anticipatory.

A few questions, if I may: has your business plateaued? Are you still doing what you were doing last year, or five years ago, even ten years ago? How would you manage your business's expectations around growth, development, and evolution if your business were your client?

When I was growing up in Northern Ireland, I came across a label applied to certain types of Scientists. They were described as "futurologists".

I was fascinated by these characters – the idea of being able to look into the future and anticipate change and what life might be life ten or twenty years from now.

To avoid stasis, you must be forward thinking.

You must be strategic with your anticipation of how you need to adjust to reflect your growth and the growth of your business in meeting anticipated need – be ahead of the turn.

Be future orientated. Be strategic in setting time aside, be it weekly or monthly, to anticipate the changes that may be coming over the horizon in your business offering, your ways of working and who you should be working with. See the future and adjust your business into a new model for a new phase – for if you continue to plant potatoes in a carrot harvest, you will get crop redundancy.

More questions for you:
- Who is helping you?
- Who is looking out for you?
- Who has the vision to help you?

To the degree that strategic anticipation is necessary in order to adopt a fluid approach to the shifting movements of the world in which you offer your services, there are times and seasons when the best person to help you make those adjustments is an objective business coach who can get alongside you and mentor / coach you on how to adapt what you offer now to what you anticipate to coming down the line ahead of you.

If this strategic thinking and planning is not your forte, seek out a business coach who can work with you to maximise what you are doing now to position yourself for the future.

Don't be caught reflecting to yourself; "I should have seen that coming".

CHAPTER 6

Leadership: What's in a Definition?

By Ian Llewellyn-Nash

By background, I am a Social Scientist. In terms of occupation, I have been an educator, a registered nurse, a Royal Naval medic, a Church Minister, and a Housing Officer. All these aspects shape who I am. When I became a leader, I somehow got lost amongst all the things that I had done. When I was asked by colleagues, what type of leader I was, the textbook definitions sounded good, yet they seemed trivial. There was a lesson I needed to learn.

Definitions – as a scientist and a nurse, there is a certain safety in definitions. They point to a reality that something is this, but not that!

When I began to become interested in people development, or personal leadership – it seemed an ideal way to go to teach 'the definition'. Yet, I soon discovered that after some 40 years of academic study into leadership, there are undoubtedly as many definitions as there are people to ask!

This presents a challenge – is leadership 'this', or is it 'that'? There are perhaps two givens; to lead is to have someone who follows: to have a follower is to have a relationship base to your leadership. In the context of a leader-follower relationship, what does your leadership look like?

If you are anything like myself, I am relatively certain that you did not wake up one morning and step into the world as any sort of leader.

You may have read books about leadership, you may have attended courses, even conferences on leadership – none of that however makes you a leader. They are certainly valuable components on the journey – but they do tend towards being 'outcome' oriented. That is, they focus on things you have done.

Leadership emerges out of the process – process enriches. Are you struggling to make sense of your leadership journey? Are you feeling unsure as to how you show up as a leader? Do folk listen to you, respond to you, even follow you?

Focus not on the tasks of leadership; they are simply the tools. Leadership is about who you are, much more than about what you do.

What will you contribute? As a leader, given the context in which you work; given your strengths, your values, your way of working – what is it you will add to that place in terms of lasting value?

Leadership is about who you are – more than what you do. Your leadership flows out of a value base. Here is a helpful activity for you to start to build your leadership – personal or professional;

Choose three feelings from the list below that you want to encourage in your leadership, or in your team.

Absorbed / Capable / Challenged / Confident / Curious / Empowered / Encouraged / Energised / Engaged / Enthusiastic / Inspired / Interested / Intrigued / Motivated / Optimistic / Receptive / Resourceful / Safe / Stimulated / Understood / Valued.

Questions – what do you currently do in your 'leading' that is likely to encourage these feelings

KAREN BURGE

BUSINESS OWNER AT
KAREN J BURGE LTD

CHAPTER 7

Is Your Marketing Message Falling on Stony Ground?

By Karen Burge

Do you know the parable of the farmer scattering his seed in the hope of a good crop? Unfortunately, some of it fell on hard ground, some seed was eaten by birds, and some blew away. I see that happen to a lot of marketing!

Most business owners want to serve 'everybody' and consequently their marketing isn't producing a good crop of customers.

The easier way to get a good crop – a solid stream of clients – is to decide on a niche. If you've never considered this, please read on, because if you discover that a niche is for you, it can transform your business.

First, never worry about missing out. Even when you clearly state whom you serve, there will still be others who'll come and ask if you can help them too. Only now, you can decide if you want them as customers!

When you decide to serve a particular section of people, you'll study and learn all about them. As you research, you'll come to understand them, their challenges and their needs. Then you see that you can provide them with the solution they're searching for. Your marketing message can now be very specific in who you help and how.

Claire is a client of mine and she's an Accountant. There are a lot of Accountants! Whenever she tried to promote her business, her marketing was like scattered seeds – falling on stony ground.

We discussed who she really wanted to work with and where her expertise lay and she decided she wanted to focus on Solicitors. She became 'The Solicitors Accountant!'

Now if she goes networking, she knows what to say. Her message is clear across her website, her social media and even her business cards.

She doesn't waste time talking to 'everybody', but when a solicitor approaches her, they immediately hear that she is the solution for them. She no longer has to sort the wheat from the chaff!

When you listen to your chosen market, you pick up their language.

You notice the words and phrases they use to describe what they're thinking, feeling and doing. You can now use these words in your marketing messages, knowing your ideal clients will instantly understand.

When you have a niche, you know exactly what your people want, and you know that you have the solution. You're the person they need, and you can describe the result you can give them. Suddenly you can create a message that's clear and very effective.

If you don't have a niche, consider whether you could. Who do you enjoy serving? Where does your expertise lie? Who would be great customers for your business? Get clear on a specific group and you can plant your marketing seeds, knowing they'll grow, instead of scattering them to the wind and that will help your business grow.

KAREN FERGUSON

BUSINESS OWNER AT
LIFETHERAPY UK
COACHING

CHAPTER 8

When Friendship and Business Collide

By Karen Ferguson

How do you deal with it when you tell a friend that you have business idea and they say that they would like to be involved?

It is all too easy to get carried away with the idea of working with someone you know, someone you have fun with and someone you may turn to when you are feeling sad or down. But that doesn't mean that they will be someone you should plan on working with. In fact, based on my experience, sometimes they are the very last people you should choose to work with, particularly if they have no experience of business, working for themselves, or worse still, if you know they can be unreliable.

It might seem like a fun idea to begin with, chatting over a glass of wine or a cup of tea as you plan what will happen, how it will work and of course how you will spend all that money. But have you stopped to think, or better still, asked them exactly what it is they can bring to the plan?

Enthusiasm is all very well, but it is not enough…

- Do they have any knowledge of the area you plan to work in?
- Are they willing and able to invest money if that is required?
- Does their future plan match yours?
- How compatible would you be if you worked together?
- What if you are proactive and they are more reactive?
- What if you have a clear end goal, but they can't see past the next few months?
- What if you are driven and determined, and they are more laid back and see what happens?

It has been my experience that working with friends is often a very bad idea, when you choose the wrong one that is, or when your friendship isn't as close or equally balanced as you may think.

I have worked with people who were friends but who were unable to see the bigger picture, who despite me being really clear that I did not want a business partnership with them, became resentful when they weren't given the recognition they thought they deserved, despite me asking exactly what they wanted from the role and how they saw their role progressing.

I've experienced bullying from someone who was angry that their invoice wasn't paid when they thought it should have been, despite me clearly putting in writing the deadline for submitting invoices and the payment dates.

When I pointed this out and showed them when their invoice had been posted, proving it could not have reached me by the deadline, they simply claimed they hadn't thought about this but never apologised for their behaviour. I lost trust in this person, and it didn't take long for both the work relationship and friendship to end.

The point here is that not everyone is the right fit for your business, not everyone has the same drive as you and not everyone should cross that line between friendship and business.

KYLIE ANDERSON

BUSINESS OWNER AT
KYLIE ANDERSON COACHING
ICONIC WEALTH
INTERNATIONAL

CHAPTER 9

It's Okay to Talk About Money!

By Kylie Anderson

Why do so many women shy away from talking about money, wanting money, charging what they are worth and shouting about their success?

At the 'Her Story Conference' for women (before COVID-19 hit) I listened to incredible stories of survival, breaking through barriers, creating their life out of lemons. It was so inspiring YET not one woman had talked about their financial success.

They avoided it
Shied away from it…

I was meant to be sharing my story on that stage. How I'd lost my brother at the age of 23. How I got married and divorced a year later, how finding out I wasn't pregnant for the second time made me stop and think seriously about my life. So much to take in… so much that, aged 27, I got up and walked away from everything.

I booked my first overseas flight and since then I've travelled to over 45 different destinations, but my travel bug needed funding! The high-flying corporate world of sales provided these funds but involved 50-hour weeks. Fast forward 12 years and I decided enough was enough. I was burnt out, emotionally and physically shattered and needed to make a change.

I got into the entrepreneurial world and found my passion again – helping other experts to break free from working 1:1 to creating an online leveraged program, preferably high ticket so that they could create more income and more freedom. YET every time I worked with other awesome female entrepreneurs with incredible knowledge, skills and expertise, they were struggling financially and I noticed that they shied away from money!

Talking about it
Wanting it
Monitoring it
Charging it

Basically giving, giving, giving and yet struggling continually themselves, surviving not thriving.

I soon realised they were not putting on their own oxygen mask first.

They had never been shown or really appreciated what the real impact of earning good money could do for them!

Because, as I keep saying, "When good women earn good money, they do good things".

When women earn good money, they make a positive impact with it. They give it back to their families, they make a positive difference in society. Yet often when women talk about wanting money, they feel guilt and shame, and when women do share their success, they are quickly and often brutally, shut down by other women! I saw someone share their success of hitting £1 million, the women who jumped on her for doing this were awful, nasty and unsupportive.

…And we wonder why we don't talk about money.

How can we change this without talking about it; by exposing it and putting it out there into the everyday stream of conversation? Money is simply a form of transaction and energy after all.

The first step is to ask yourself, "what do I truly want?" get clarity around two core numbers:

- Get your 'life covered', the costs of all the basics of rent, mortgage, food bills etc. that you need to cover each month.
- Create your 'lifestyle' figure. Add in at least 2-3 things annually that you really want to have in order to live your best life.

Add these two figures together and there's your annual and monthly target. Now ask yourself, is your business set up to achieve this? If not, you have some work to do!

It's time for women to feel elated by earning good money' It's time for us to feel genuinely excited about charging what we're worth, to stop feeling guilty about having money, to celebrate each other's success!

Here's to your financial success.

LAURA BILLINGHAM

BUSINESS OWNER AT
L&G ASSOCIATES LTD
WORD WITCH

CHAPTER 10

Love Your Business

By Laura Billingham

We're all familiar with the adage, "you have to love yourself" – it's almost become the catchphrase of the 21st Century…well that and "Google it"! But what about the way you earn your living, your job, your business – can you honestly say you love that too, or do you see it just as a means to an end? A way to earn enough money so you can retire and live a lazy life!

Let me tell you a story about me and how I ended up LOVING my business and the work I do. I wasn't always so in love with it – heck no!

In fact, when I first set up on my own (this time around anyway), I quickly realised the path I had chosen really wasn't rocking my world – in fact, it was making me miserable.

You see, I had opted to buy into a Virtual PA franchise (and it wasn't cheap!), partly because it seemed 'the safer thing to do' and partly because of assurances and promises the franchise company made to me, and others.

Having had various office manager type roles over the years, I believed helping someone else run their business was all I could do…talk about a limiting belief.

I actually thoroughly enjoyed the training which was part of the 'package', but the promised guaranteed clients never appeared, and I quickly realised that to people on the network scene I was part of, I was 'just a secretary'. I know, I know – there is absolutely nothing wrong with secretarial work…it just isn't me!

Fast forward a couple of years to 2018, I was still just going through the motions with the business – and then I started to do more internal self-development work…and POW! Literally overnight, I changed my thoughts and beliefs to what I really wanted to be – a WRITER. By the end of that year, I had completed a novel, met a certain lady by the name of Sharon Brown (some of you may know her too "grin") and switched my business to being that of a content creator.

Over time I've built up a steady flow of clients, other business owners who want me to write their web content, social media and blog posts, and I coined the phrase – "giving business owners a written voice". These smaller pieces of work have developed into ghost-writing entire books for business owners who lack either the time or inclination to create their own material. I've even found the time to publish another book of my own, this time an anthology of short stories all written in May 2021 during one of the lockdowns.

So, my message to all of you, is to love your business; love what you do and I promise you it won't feel like work. You'll want to show up every single day and give your very best to your clients, your business AND yourself.

CHAPTER 11

It's All About Words

By Laura Billingham

When you first start your business, you are probably very aware that you need a logo and some idea of colours, fonts and imagery. You'll be told by designers and marketing experts that you need to create 'your business brand' (or your personal brand) and you'll be bombarded by offers to create your artwork, logo, images and website.

You'll be advised to use this brand image in everything you do – from email campaigns to social media, and website, and physical things like store fronts, letterheads, and business cards.

And all of this is absolutely great! You will start to get recognised, prospective customers and clients will check you out...BUT what happens when those prospects visit your website, open the email, or read the letter and the written words they see don't match your carefully created brand?

Think of a brand as a personality. For example, your image, branding suggests a young, vibrant, energetic, brand personality – think Apple, Nike, Amazon – but your copy is flowery, old fashioned and boring. Or you have carefully cultivated a 'high end' business brand – think Gucci, Chanel, Cartier – but your copy is grammatically poor and more representative of 'hip hop' than haute couture!

The words you use within your brand are just as important as your logo and other visuals, and yet they often seem to be the last thing a business owner considers.

The website designer may create a fabulous looking site for you, but not all website designers are great at copy – especially the smaller companies who are (usually) more affordable for a start-up business. You may be asked to create your own content, but if you aren't confident in your writing skills, how comfortable will you feel to see your words 'written large for all to see'?

The problem is, first impressions count, so if your words don't match the brand image you are trying to create, your business will come across as confused and inauthentic – as if you don't know who you are or what you are doing (when of course you do…don't you?).

SO, HOW DO YOU GET IT RIGHT? HOW DO YOU CREATE WRITTEN CONTENT THAT MATCHES YOUR BRAND?

1. Ensure you know what your brand personality and message actually is – and if you don't know, figure it out quickly!
2. Whether you personally, or a contractor, are responsible, ensure the written content matches your brand personality across ALL mediums…be consistent.
3. Make sure you check your spelling and grammar (all word processing applications include spell and grammar checks… a top tip is to use the 'read aloud' function as this helps with the 'flow' of the words).
4. DO NOT PLAGIARISE!
5. Employ a specialist! (but of course, as a content writer I would say that wouldn't I?)

Finally, always remember – words are very powerful, so use them carefully!

MARK TERRELL

BUSINESS OWNER AT
THE RELUCTANT LEADER
ACADEMY
THE MOTIVATED BUSINESS
CLUB

CHAPTER 12

Running Out of Steam

By Mark Terrell

Running a business takes energy so you need to make sure you have plenty of it, especially when you hit those bumps in the road that inevitably appear. Thinking of your business as a journey is a useful way to remember that it's not all about the end destinations, we also need the right vehicle to get there and keep topping up the tank with the right fuel.

I joined our family retail business straight from school. I had spent most of my school holiday working in the business and really enjoyed it. I enjoyed school and was tempted to stay on to take A Levels, but my father had other ideas. The business was growing and he needed help.

I soon realised that working full time in the business was a lot different to a few hours during the school holidays. I decided to step up and take some responsibility. The first thing I decided to put my stamp on was the fresh produce section, buying the right products, displaying and pricing to maximise sales.

'Retail is detail', is what they say so getting the display right was important, using the different colours to create a tempting display and then seeing the result in sales was exhilarating. I moved on to other departments in the store and each time putting my creative side to use and putting my own stamp on how things were done.

As time went by, I started to take on more responsibility and eventually ended up in charge of the day to day running of the store, and managing people became the biggest part of my day. I'd never had any formal training to manage people so I led the only way I knew, by supporting and encouraging.

When I look back on my energy levels at each step in my journey, I realise now where I get my energy from and what takes energy from me. Being creative and solving problems using new ideas generally gives me energy especially when it's something that I regard as worthwhile and that makes a difference.

What doesn't give me energy is having the responsibility in managing people, it's not that I can't do it, I just don't find it fulfilling. This is the most important lesson I learnt, do what gives you energy most of the time and limit the time you spend on things that sap your energy.

If you're running a business, it's easy to fall into the trap of doing all the things nobody else wants to do, especially if you're good at them. Take time to think about the role you are creating for yourself in your business and having a vision of what that looks like will help to prevent you ending up in a place you don't want to be.

MARK WOOD

BUSINESS OWNER AT
MY NLP WORKS LIMITED

CHAPTER 13

Want More Clients?

By Mark Wood

So, you have a business, and things are going great! You sell your product or service, and get a good price, but there are those leads that just seem to pass you by, the 'ones that got away' kind of client. What can you do to grab those missed opportunities? How can you turn that around?

Firstly, you need to know that you're pitching to the right people, at the right time, and in the right location. Check out your perfect client, what their needs are, what it is they want but don't yet have, and put yourself in their shoes. See what they see, hear what they hear, feel what they're feeling about their need. Then ask yourself this question:

Does my product or service fulfil that need?'

That might sound obvious, but think about Pareto's principle, or as some might say, the 80/20 rule.

We spend 80% of our time chasing 20% of the leads we think are going to work with us, instead of cutting our losses and investing our time into those who will come through and be a profitable client. Look for a 'No', rather than a 'yes'.

Second, how often do we make contact with a prospective client, and forge ahead with our sales pitch without listening to what the client says? When we talk, we utilise things called Modalities.

So, what are Modalities? Well, they are those senses which we use to gain information about our world, and include Sight, Sound, Feelings, Smell and Taste.

We all have one or more of these as our preferred modality, and this leaks into our everyday language. We've all heard someone say, 'I can see a clearer picture now', or 'that's crystal clear to me'. How about 'Sounds great to me!' or 'I hear what you're saying', and how about 'I have a great feeling about this project', or 'this is a great foundation to start from?'

By listening to what people are saying, we can then modify our own language to utilise those same modalities, and by doing so, begin to build up a stronger rapport with the other person.

People like people who are like themselves. If we know someone is using Visual (Sight) language, we can respond appropriately, e.g. 'How does that look to you?' Likewise, Auditory (Sound) language can sound like this. 'Hear something you like; does it sound good to you?' And for Kinaesthetic (Feelings) we could say, 'Does that feel good to you, are we hitting your requirements?'

We also use our internal self-talk (Auditory Digital) and can say, 'Do you think this is a good solution for you?', or 'you know this makes sense'.

So, listen more carefully to what others are saying, and figure out what is your own preferred Modality, so that you can become more aware of how you speak to others. Now, go close that client!

MARTIN SHARP

BUSINESS OWNER AT
WAXTIE LTD
SHARP FIT FOR LIFE

CHAPTER 14

A Comedy of Errors Ends in Death

By Martin Sharp

Do you know that feeling, where you try do things right and whatever happens, doesn't seem to go the way you planned it?

And you'll know the phrase, "You win some, you learn some!" Yet do you actually learn?

After seven years, I'm cashing up the virtual till, shutting the virtual windows, and locking the virtual door for the last time on one of my businesses. It is time to say goodbye. Not because I am dead, or any living being has been brought to a swift and premature demise, but because I realised the business was no longer serving me. It had become a drain on my time, my money and my own health.

It reminded me of one of the critical things that as a business owner, you need to have planned from the start – your exit strategy.

Because in reality, you only have seven ways to exit a business:

- Your death
- Your expulsion
- Your ill health
- You lose your marbles
- You liquidate
- You keep it in the family
- You sell

When I've spoken with business owners, they think about the last two, with aspirations of building something to pass on or sell later in life to reap the rewards of their hard work.

The thing is, it is not always going to end that way and you need to be thinking about the other five ways…

You may realise a loss, but this is not always a bad thing. If you can capitalise it before closing the business you can use it as part of your tax allowance. As with everything to do with your business finances, you need to speak with your Accountant. Make sure you have a fabulous relationship with them. If your Accountant doesn't initially feel expensive, you only see them once a year and they don't suggest ways of maximising your money, you are with the wrong Accountant!

Reflect on what you have learned, people you've met since you started the business, the experiences that may not have opened up. The experiences that may never open up. The loss is part of your education, so make it count – after all, it is a foolish man who doesn't learn from his mistakes.

You can free up capital to use elsewhere, yes. If there are assets in the business, you need to find a buyer.

Assets aren't always physical items like property or machinery. It could be intellectual property, or a relationship, perhaps you could help other businesses by introducing them to suppliers or customers.

Did you systemise something that makes things easier, cheaper, more predictable? Can you help other businesses learn from your mistakes?

Then there is always the next adventure. Having realised the effect running major transformations for global enterprises from my micro consultancy firm was having on my own wellbeing, I'm now concentrating my effort on Physique and Lifestyle coaching for business owners. You never know, I may find a way to fix the obesity crisis.

CHAPTER 15

Growth

By Martin Sharp

Have you ever felt that there is even more than you are currently achieving?

Perhaps you feel like you've hit a plateau. You're struggling to make any meaningful move forward.

Failing to become more than you currently are today may give you some issues. Potentially regarding your income or performance, or fulfilling your life goals, making you feel unhappy, miserable, frustrated or angry while you're looking for ways to push beyond the barrier as you can see that thing in front of you, but you are unable to reach it yet.

Yet imagine, when you break through that limitation, you're reaching new goals, making things happen, and it is all working well. You are so happy because you've got this freedom and flexibility, you've got your finances in order, and the main thing is you're completely congruent with who you are and are happier for it.

Now you may have been taught that failure is not an option. That is one of NASA's famous quotes and a common thread going through many areas of people's lives. Through schooling, having to pass exams to progress. Having to win awards to be recognised. Having to be great at sport, included in team selection. Then also into employment where failure to comply with rules, successfully implement a project or run within budget is non-negotiable, which can be a career-limiting experience if you fail. There are tests and evaluations, like your driving test or applying for a mortgage, that they're looking for you not to fail.

This drive to constantly succeed without failure puts enormous and unnatural pressure on you that isn't needed.

That said, failure is an option! Failure is life's way of giving you feedback, a point to show you which direction you need to put more effort into to succeed and if you don't fail, you can be in the position of not pushing yourself hard enough to grow. Fail so you can grow happens naturally in so many areas of life.

If you're not pushing limits inside your business to find out where boundaries are, you may find you wake up one day no longer having a business because your clients no longer see you as cutting edge or providing a service they need.

Maybe what was an innovative service or product has become a commodity, and therefore you have to fight every day to maintain your current position.

With your own body, if you're finding that you're no longer progressing with your goal of losing weight, gaining muscle, and improving endurance, speed or stamina, maybe it is because you're not pushing your body hard enough to make the adaptions it needs. So, by not failing, you're not giving your body what it needs to build to survive and thrive. Sometimes you have to fail to be able to break through that plateau if you do want to make something better.

SUCCESS MAY FEEL NICE IN THE MOMENT, THOUGH GROWING THROUGH FAILURE AND CELEBRATING MANY WINS ALONG THE JOURNEY WILL HELP KEEP YOU GOING FOREVER!

MELITTA CAMPBELL

BUSINESS OWNER AT
MELITTA CAMPBELL
BUSINESS COACH FOR
WOMEN

CHAPTER 16

How to Attract More Clients with One Sentence

By Melitta Campbell

As a Business Coach, I consistently see one business challenge stand out above all others; having the ability to attract enough clients to earn a predictable income.

For many entrepreneurs, this has been compounded following the COVID-19 chaos. But the good news is, there is one strategy I believe can help business owners in all industries to rise above this challenge – having a clear and meaningful Value Proposition (VP).

What is a Value Proposition?

Your VP describes the benefits a customer can expect from your products and services. While the statement may be quite simple, the process of arriving at your VP can take considerable research and reflection. You'll know you've got your proposition right when you present it and get an "OMG I need this – tell me more!" response over the. More common, "Oh, that's nice".

Your VP is just the first stage in attracting your ideal clients, but sets the scene for your entire client relationship, making it a crucial step to get right – yet many business owners stumble at this stage.

AVOID A 'ONE VP FITS ALL APPROACH'.

How to create or update your Value Proposition:
Your VP has two sides.

On one side, you'll want to explore the value your product or service offers, and in what ways this is different or better than the competition. On the other, you'll want to understand your customers' challenges in depth, and how you solve their problem in new or different ways.

Once you know this, look for where these two sides align, and communicate those benefits that are most meaningful to your prospective clients, that position you ahead of your competitors.

Avoid this Common Error:
When creating their VP, many entrepreneurs get excited and share all the benefits their business creates. Don't fall into this trap. Take time to discover which of your benefits resonates most with your prospects.

Also avoid a 'one VP fits all approach'. Most businesses need a different VP for each client segment.

It takes more time, but your ability to attract more of your ideal clients will more than justify the extra effort.

A quick-start Value Proposition Framework:
While it can take time to get your VP right, here is a simple framework to get you started.

I provide *(add your product or service)* for *(add your ideal client)* to help them *(add in a powerful benefit that you offer)*, which means they can *(add in a result of what you do)*. Once you have your VP tried, tested and ready to go, share it with your team and partners, and in all your messaging – its power lies in its consistent use.

A final tip – BELIEVE IT!
When sharing your VP with others, make sure you 100% believe in the results you offer.

People will pick up on any doubt, which will undermine your efforts. If you're not yet there, use gratitude and affirmations based on your VP to build your confidence. Then enjoy meaningful interactions with your prospects, and watch the sales roll in.

MILA JOHANSEN

BUSINESS OWNER AT
FROM PEN TO PUBLISHED

CHAPTER 17

Hiring Your Dream Team

By Mila Johansen

Whether you hire one person, dozens, or hundreds, assembling the right team is essential to the success of your business. I have run several businesses with one to fifty employees. The secret I have found to building a successful team is finding the right person for each job. Sometimes it even comes down to personality.

For instance, I have been to offices where the person greeting the public is cheerful and makes everything easy and effortless. Conversely, I have seen the wrong person sitting in that seat, who is introverted and makes you feel like you are interrupting their day. I try to hire the person who is a natural fit for the position.

Finding the right people doesn't always mean hiring the most qualified or experienced. Sometimes, a person who is fresh and eager can be trained to be a valuable, loyal addition to any team. In fact, there are entire companies who prefer to train their employees from the ground up.

For many businesses, the concept of training all employees to do everything has the advantage of making everyone interchangeable, which can be an asset when employees are absent for any reasons or leave the company. That approach works for certain types of businesses such as copy and print shops, sales in online or brick and mortar stores, restaurants and many more.

Other companies may need to hire experts in the various positions that need to be filled. For instance, almost every business could benefit from a talented social media person on staff to conduct their online presence and online advertising.

With the onslaught of the pandemic, it is sometimes difficult to find enough employees to fill the positions. Each company will need to come up with enticing incentives for a prospect to consent to joining a team. Incentives could be anything from incremental increases in pay, to workplace perks like complimentary food or onsite day-care, to four-day work weeks and optional telecommuting.

I read several articles about ten years ago predicting that one half of the workforce would be telecommuting by the year 2020. I wonder if it is happening naturally as predicted, or did the pandemic accelerate the phenomenon?

I hire people who may know more than me in certain areas, to fill in my own knowledge and talent gaps. Often, I will take an enthusiastic person over an experienced one and take the time to train them. To my delight, they often surpass me. I have been very fortunate to hire excellent employees who, in the end, tell me what's going on.

Through respect, accountability, and trust, I have been able to keep employees happily working for me – sometimes for decades. We work together as a team, and I love handing off entire projects for the right person to accomplish. As a neophyte business owner, decades ago, I had to learn to delegate and the secret to delegating is to hire the right people.

MONIKA MATEJA

BUSINESS OWNER AT
LIVE WELL COACHING LTD

CHAPTER 18

Focus Will Get You There

By Monika Mateja

I woke up one day all sweaty (no it was not a menopausal hot flash). I was dreaming vividly about travelling. Not about exotic countries and wonderful destinations, it was rather a nightmare of being lost in a labyrinth of small and narrow streets and passages. Each one had a fork-like junction, so I had to choose which path to take. It was a tough choice, because how would I know which one is right? Neither looked appealing and both were very similar. Applying reason only, did not feel right so I used my intuition to choose the one I felt would be for me.

Making a choice like that left me anxious and almost immediately regretting my decision. Have you ever felt like that? Yeah, quite a common feeling.

I am not sure about you, but I had the strangest dreams in this pandemic. I think the lack of real and varied experiences allowed my brain to almost create an alternative world for me to have some fun.

I started my business in August 2019 after quitting my career in corporate after 15 years. Little did I know what was coming in 2020, well nobody knew. I started well with the first client in September and then others followed later. I also did successful cooking workshops and supper clubs. However, it was not how I imagined it. I thought I would have a constant flow of clients who want to invest their time and money into their health. The feast and famine cycle is well known in the coaching industry, where you have dry periods without any potential clients. Nobody knows you, and your message is not consistent because you lack clarity and want to try what works. You probably spend around 70% of your time in marketing and 30% coaching – not something you want to do as a Coach.

I tried a lot of different things, but the key was to understand what kind of lifestyle I wanted to have. What do I want to do in this business? How do I want to work and with whom? It took me some time to get that clarity. A lot of us want to do great things, help people, and earn a good living. However, it is hard to understand your own self-limiting beliefs, as well as balancing your lifestyle and demands of the family, with your dream to be more and do more in this world, without detriment to your own health.

It is about choosing the path you feel most connected to. It may not be the best looking, but your intuition never lies. Through all this time I repeated to myself, "stay in your lane", which was not easy as the pandemic hit. One path will definitely take you faster to your destination, but it does not mean that you cannot stop and look around, reflect, and rethink. It is all about the journey.

NICOLA MATTHEWS

BUSINESS OWNER AT
NICOLA MATTHEWS
ONLINE BUSINESS
MANAGEMENT

CHAPTER 19

Why Every Business Should Set KPI's

By Nicola Matthews

How's your business doing?

As a business owner, you're probably used to hearing that question, often by someone making polite conversation rather than out of genuine interest! But do you really know how your business is doing?

Your financial accounts will give you a good indication, but they don't give the whole picture. You should monitor your business performance on an ongoing basis, and Key Performance Indicators (KPIs) are an excellent way to do so. As well as a snapshot of where you currently are, they can also help develop a roadmap for getting to where you want to be.

Key Performance Indicators (KPIs):

KPIs are a set of measurables, which give a clear picture of how well a business is achieving its objectives. As the business owner, you determine what you want to measure, so it's important that your own objectives are well established.

Measuring and recording information for the sake of it is of little benefit!

Deciding what to measure:

Start with your objectives and establish what you need to do to achieve them. Then decide what you need to measure to ensure you're on track. It's a good idea to limit the number of KPIs to just a couple for each objective. Too many will be overwhelming, and you'll end up spending more time collecting and analysing your data than acting upon it. Too many will also dilute your efforts – it's far better to focus on improving in a couple of areas instead of tackling everything at once. KPIs can change and adapt as your business evolves.

What to do with your KPIs:

You've decided what you want to achieve, how you're going to achieve it and what you need to measure in order to get there, now what?

Firstly, you need to make sure you have an easy to use format for displaying your KPIs. There are plenty of templates available online, so find one that works for you, or design your own.

Secondly, try to automate as much of the data collection process as possible. If you're relying on human input to gather the information you need and them to collate it into a meaningful format, not only will this be time consuming, but you also run the risk of it being side-lined or only done sporadically.

Thirdly, monitor your KPIs regularly. This might be weekly or monthly, but it needs to be frequently enough to see if the actions you take are having an effect.

It's also wise to regularly check that the KPIs you're recording are still valuable in achieving your current business goals.

What KPIs DON'T do:

KPIs are a valuable business tool but they have limitations. They can only be used for quantitative data, which doesn't always give the full picture. KPI's need to be viewed in the context of the whole business and don't forget, the act of measuring in itself doesn't help in achieving your objectives. It can only help you identify the effectiveness of the actions you take.

CHAPTER 20

Outsource to Upscale

By Nicola Matthews

If you want to scale up your business, there comes a point when you realise you can't do it all on your own. Maybe you've looked at the option of taking on employees but have been left confused by legalities or put off by the potential cost.

A more flexible option is to consider outsourcing. Where you engage the services of a freelancer or contractor to undertake work for you.

The beauty of this is that you only pay for the work that is done via an hourly rate, a set project fee, or on a retainer basis.

What to outsource:

There are three main aspects of running a business that people usually outsource:

- Things they don't enjoy doing. This varies between individuals but is often the more mundane activities that don't generate income but still have to be done.

- Things they don't have time to do, like posting regularly on social media channels.
- Things they don't have the correct skills to do, for example bookkeeping as their business grows, or website maintenance.

How to outsource successfully:

So, you've decided to take the plunge and outsource. How do you ensure you're set up for success?

- Don't leave it until you're swamped, plan ahead. This is crucial! If you wait until you are at capacity, you won't have the time to effectively hand over the jobs that need doing.
- Establish what you want to outsource before seeking support.
- Be realistic about what you can pass on to someone else and ensure your business systems are set up to support this. As a business owner, you may hold lots of information in your head, but to delegate, it needs to be accessible to others.
- Be specific in your requirements. So often, you'll see someone post on social media along the lines of 'help! I think I need a VA!' Can anyone recommend someone?' They will then invariably be inundated with responses and will have to sift through them all, only to find that none are suitable.

- Ask for recommendations.
- Don't be afraid to let go. This is often the most challenging part for business owners, but it's an essential step in your business growth.
- Set up a meeting to discuss your needs, but remember, this is not an interview! This is an opportunity to find out if you are a good fit for each other.
- Set a test task to see whether you can work well together.
- Establish your lines of communication, how often you expect to be contacted and by which method.
- Sign a contract! This is for the protection of all parties in case anything goes wrong.

Outsourcing can be the key to scaling up your business, freeing up your time to concentrate on what you do best. Done well, you'll wonder how you ever managed without the support.

CHAPTER 21

How to: Use Email Marketing

By Nicola Matthews

Email marketing, is it something you should be doing in your business? The answer is a definite YES!

Here's why:

- Nearly 90% of adults use email
- Your email list is yours and, unlike followers on social media, you control your list
- You can choose exactly who you're marketing to, and tailor different offers and messages to different groups.
- You can assess the effectiveness of your email marketing at an individual level – what each person opens and acts upon

How do you go about making it work for you? It's not as daunting as you might think!

Build your email list:

- Offer a lead magnet – something that you give away for free, such as an eBook or a template, in exchange for their email address.
- Be really clear about what they're signing up to and make sure the lead magnet is relevant to your business.
- State what they will be receiving going forward and ensure you follow relevant data protection regulations (such as GDPR)

Choose an Email Marketing Service (provider):

There are lots to choose from and features vary.

Essentially, all will allow you to:

- Store your email list
- Send bulk marketing emails
- Ensure you comply with GDPR and provide some level of analytics to monitor the effectiveness of your campaigns.

Providers such as Mailchimp and Mailerlite offer a free service for a limited number of subscribers.

Others charge regardless of the size of your list but may offer more functionality.

Create interesting and relevant content:

Make your emails friendly and engaging, imagine you're writing to just one person, rather than hundreds or thousands. A good subject line is essential – you want to entice your reader to open the email, but don't use clickbait, this will ultimately frustrate your reader and you run the risk of being flagged as spam.

On the subject of spam, make sure you send your emails at a frequency your audience will be comfortable with.

Ensure you comply with local data protection regulations:

In a nutshell, this means making sure people actively opt in to receiving your emails, ensuring that it is easy for them to unsubscribe if they no longer wish to receive them, and keeping their data safe.

Analyse:

The final step in the process is to evaluate how well your emails are performing.

The main metrics your email marketing service should provide are:

- *Open rates* (what percentage of recipients opened the email)
- *Click through rates* (how many of them clicked on links within the email)

- *Unsubscribes* (how many unsubscribed either before or after opening the email).

Analysing these figures should give you an indication of just how useful and relevant your emails are to your audience, allowing you to modify and tailor future campaigns.

That's it! Five simple steps to starting and maintaining an effective email marketing campaign.

CHAPTER 22

How to: Fall in Love with your Business Again

By Nicola Matthews

Remember how you felt when you first started your business? It was like embarking on a new relationship. The combination of nerves and excitement, wanting to spend every waking minute on it. Even the most mundane aspect was thrilling – do you recall the buzz of preparing your first invoice?

But somewhere down the line, the passion starts to wane. Boredom sets in. Is it time to call it quits?

Before you decide to kiss your business goodbye, try these tips to help bring the passion back.

Remember why you started

Think back to when you first started, and the reason for setting up your own business. Maybe you had a calling to help others, or perhaps you simply wanted the independence and flexibility of being your own boss.

Whatever the reason, remind yourself why you set out on this path in the first place. Celebrate the journey you've been on so far and recognise every little milestone you've achieved along the way.

Ditch the dull stuff

Many business owners reach a point where they find themselves bogged down with the things they hate doing. Whether that's social media, or doing the accounts, we all have those things that we'd rather not do.

Make a list of these. Are they essential? If they aren't, stop doing them!

It sounds obvious, but many continue doing these tasks simply because they feel they should.

If they are essential, then outsourcing and automation are your friends. Make sure you document the processes involved so that you can easily hand these tasks to someone else.

Go all in!

Sometimes the best way to start loving your business is to change your mindset. Instead of viewing it with negativity, make a conscious choice to put all your energy into it.

Develop ambitious plans for the future – after all, it's your business so you get to control where it goes.

Collaborate with others with complementary businesses. Working with others can bring new perspectives and fresh ideas, and potentially open up new markets to you.

Seek new opportunities or develop your skill set, learn something new or deepen your knowledge on a particular aspect of your business.

Lastly, don't be afraid to spend. Invest wisely in the right tools, training and delegation, and your business will repay you well.

Re-evaluate

Finally, take a good look at your business. Are you just frustrated with the humdrum, or have you truly fallen out of love with it? Have you deviated from your original path and ended up going in a different direction? If this isn't working for you, then get yourself back on track.

Sometimes however, there's no going back. If so, there's no shame in giving it up and starting afresh if your business is no longer bringing you joy. Much like any relationship, you'll know when it's time to say goodbye.

PAM EDWARDS

BUSINESS OWNER AT
PHOENIX RISING SERVICES

CHAPTER 23

How Do You Get Started in Business?

By Pam Edwards

Many people would love to start their own business and get away from the restrictions and uncertainty of being stuck in a never-ending cycle of being undervalued, underpaid and always at the risk of redundancy.

So why don't more people take the plunge and go for it?

There are many reasons, but I think the biggest one is they are scared of getting it wrong, they don't want to crash and burn. That, of course, is perfectly understandable when you don't know anything about the business of being in business.

Creating a successful, long term business is about so much more than just being great at what you do. However, even with the very best ideas, you can't be successful if you don't lay strong foundations, do the necessary ground work first and make sure you really know WHY you want to turn this idea into a business.

Creating your own business is a daunting task but when you take the necessary steps and ask the necessary questions, you will gain a great deal of clarity which will help to make all the later steps much easier.

Here's a few pointers to get you started:

1. What do you want to do?
2. Why do you want to do it?

hint: it is crucial that you really know the answer here so keep asking. Be totally honest in your answers until you get to the core reason.

3. How are you going to deliver your services /products?
4. When do you want to launch your new business?
5. Know your 3 Budgets:

- ·Survival (household costs),
- ·Living (nice to have but not essential)
- ·Business Costs.

It is crucial to know your figures and you must be honest and scrupulous about this. If you don't know your budgets, how will you know if you are charging the right fees for your products and services? How will you know if you're making profits / breaking even or making a loss? You must make sure you create enough revenue to cover at least your Survival and Business Costs every month to avoid getting into debt.

6. PLAN, PLAN, PLAN

Map out on paper exactly where you want to be in 12 months' time, then track back and determine where you need to be at 9, 6 and 3 months in order to achieve your 12-month goals.

Include all you will offer together with anticipated revenues for each item.

There is no doubt that running your own business is challenging and exciting BUT we must be realistic and understand the importance of doing the groundwork properly.

It really is worth the effort of soul searching and planning, as it will help you see where things are going right – or wrong. The bumps and challenges can be overcome more effectively by being proactive rather than reactive. Things do go wrong sometimes, but if you've done your planning it will be easier to get back on track and re-focus on your long term goals.

PHIL GREGORY

BUSINESS OWNER AT
PEAK DISTRICT SEO

CHAPTER 24

Making Your Website Work for You

By Phil Gregory

Your business has a website, right? Is it good to look at? Does it bring in the leads and sales? Do customers call because they found your website?

If the answer to those questions is no, you'll want to read on.

Doesn't it frustrate you that you've already spent thousands of pounds on your website, and it's not paying its way? Think of your website as an employee. You wouldn't just hire a new employee, sit them in a corner and leave them alone, hoping that somehow they suddenly started making you money.

Websites, like employees, need regular reviews. Their work needs monitoring and changes need to be made when their performance is below par.

SEO Audits

A great way to gauge the performance of your website is to book an SEO audit.

SEO (Search Engine Optimisation) is the task of finetuning your website so that you are easily found when your customers search for you. Basically, the path to making your website do what it's meant to do, grow your audience, and increase your bottom line.

SEO is not a quick fix. Unless your website is tiny, it can't be done overnight, in a week, month or even a year. SEO is an ongoing process of marketing; done right, it will provide long-term stability and growth for your revenue.

With the right SEO partner, growing your online presence can be a comparatively easy and exciting journey.

Getting started

Get your website audited.

Find an SEO company that will investigate the following:

- Computer and mobile performance
- Ranking against your competitors for key terms
- Content quality and relevance in the eyes of Google

Most UK SEO companies will offer some form of an audit. The prices can differ dramatically. Like most things in life, buy cheap, pay twice, but the most expensive companies don't always deliver the very best results, so it's worth talking to a few to see who suits your needs best.

Whether your audit is a document or a video, you will gain an idea of just how much work your website needs to be consistently on page one of the search results.

Agree a monthly or yearly fee. Avoid anyone who offers a fixed price, one-off piece of work.

The search results are ever changing and you'll need to respond accordingly.

Get onboard with the process

Commit to understanding the process. Working together can achieve the desired results. Hungry companies who offer their expert knowledge on content and ask questions about stats and targets invariably outperform those who just sit back.

Finally, read the reviews. Trusted SEO companies will have reviews. The voices of past clients should give you a feel for who you are dealing with.

PHIL HORROD

BUSINESS OWNER AT
WORKLIFE180 COACHING

CHAPTER 25

Are you charging the right price?

By Phil Horrod

It's an impossible question to answer.

There's actually no such thing as a 'right price'.

There is, however, a range of prices for any given product or service, along which you can choose the level of pricing you decide is appropriate for your particular business.

You can choose to be low priced, in order to attract a high volume of clients (think Aldi in the world of supermarkets). Alternatively, you can choose to be at the premium end of the pricing spectrum, as a strategy to maximise your profits (think Waitrose in our supermarket example).

You can of course choose anywhere in between these two, depending on the criteria you use to make your choice.

Perhaps you have a close competitor who you want to undercut. Useful if you're service isn't particularly unique and you serve a highly competitive market place.

Possibly you need a particular income per hour, if that's the way you choose to charge for you services. Or maybe you've taken a more scientific approach, calculating all your costs, then adding on the amount you want to make as profit. More entrepreneurs should adopt this latter approach, even if just to verify they are actually recovering all their costs and making a true profit.

Economists have lots of fancy theories about pricing. However, in the end, it really just comes down to two main types of pricing strategy.

1. Cost – plus, where all your costs are calculated and a profit margin added on top, or
2. Market-based, where your pricing is based on the prevailing rates of your competitors.

In an ideal world, the best approach to take is to use a market-based approach first, then to verify this pricing level, by calculating what your profitability is by using the cost-plus approach as a cross-check.

Part of the reason I suggest this, is that many entrepreneurs often forget to include various elements of their costs in their calculations. These should include all your normal living expenses, like rent / mortgage costs, energy and other utility bills, your weekly shopping bill, pension fund contributions, not to mention needing to pay the tax man your Income Tax and National Insurance contributions, or your corporation tax bill, depending on your chosen legal business structure.

Conversely, if you've taken a cost-plus approach to your pricing as your starting point and come up with a price based on the recovery of all your costs and your profit margin, how do you know if that makes you cheap or expensive, compared to your competitors? In this situation, it's still important to verify this by way of comparison to your competition. Only then will you know if you're undercutting them, possibly missing out on potential revenue, or are way above them, potentially missing out on securing a greater number of clients.

Despite all this, in reality, there is a right level of pricing for your business after all. It's simply the level that your clients are prepared to pay you for your product or service! Just like the value of a house, or a second-hand car. In the real world, anything is only worth what someone else is prepared to pay for it

RAMONA STRONACH

BUSINESS OWNER AT
TAP YOUR POSSIBLE

CHAPTER 26

EFT for Business

By Ramona Stronach

How do you inspire yourself when it comes to your business?

How much time do you devote to really listen to what you yearn for from your business?

For me, it is about connection to energy. I see my business as an extension of myself – of my own energy, my values, desires and ambitions. I am in a relationship with my business and this has helped me view it as a partner in life:

- A partner who will provide for me.
- A partner who will help me serve others in a deeply authentic way.
- A partner that will enable me to have more free time in my life to focus on pursuits that bring me joy and aliveness.

Have you ever considered your business in these terms?
When I am holding space for another as an Emotional Freedom Technique (EFT) Practitioner, the space is sacred. It benefits

both parties. So, on days where enthusiasm is waning or unhelpful thoughts surface, I engage with how my business and I feel through tapping on the body's meridian points. This shifts stuck energy that can block our wisdom and creativity. As I tap, I let my business know how I am feeling, how I want to feel about it as if I was having a conversation with a significant other.

I take the time to witness my business's needs, where its energy wants to flow, what it wants to express and what ideas it has for itself. I give it space to have a voice, just as I would a client. I may also take pen to paper and write to my business, as I would a partner, seeking their opinion. My business, after all, is going to look after me on so many levels – personally, financially, and professionally. So I truly want to invest in this relationship.

The 'in flow' energy I have experienced using EFT (commonly known as tapping), has helped me take inspired actions to launch my business, 'Tap Your Possible'.

I don't know about you, but I want to build my business from this place of flow, not from anxiety and stress. I want my business to reflect my heart's deepest vision, and I know it will because I take action as a result of going within, listening to my innermost feelings and tapping on them. Tapping enables us to find a space within very quickly, so that we can feel into our place of wisdom and allow easeful, creative energy to flow through us and all of our business endeavours. This, for me, is inspiring. I dare you to try it out.

I wish whoever reads this a beautiful business journey.

SAM DOSSA

BUSINESS OWNER AT CREATE YOUR DESTINY

CHAPTER 27

How Emotional Intelligence is Good for Business

By Sam Dossa

Many times, it's the circumstances and our beliefs formed over time due to exposure to culture, religion, etc, that decide how we feel about our most significant events in life. Mental health is directly related to how we feel about certain things and how intensely we feel about them.

No feeling is useless or out of place. Every emotion has its value and significance, the goal is to understand and identify them so that they can become constructive and manageable.

Emotional Intelligence has these five elements:

Knowing one's emotions:

Self-awareness is the ability to evaluate our own emotions and understand the impact they can have on oneself. Through self-awareness one can identify their own strengths and areas to improve. This alone can provide somebody with mental health issues to appreciate their current position.

Managing Editions:

The ability to regulate emotion could be mandatory for dealing with mental health. Our emotions can vary throughout the day and their very nature can show whether we can control these emotions. When experiencing mental health challenges, it can be deemed that minor issues become major ones due to inability to cope.

Regulating emotion is not easy and is something that should be practised consistently. Common strategies to regulate emotion include setting goals, mindfulness, deep breathing, meditation, positive self-talk, listening to music and reflective practice.

Motivating Yourself:

A persistent influx of motivation is a characteristic symptom of happiness. Also, happiness can be increased or prolonged when a person experiences a greater desire to complete certain tasks or engage in regular activities.

Recognising Emotions in Others:

Social situations can be handled efficiently when one understands what people are thinking and feeling. It is important to have good social connections for great physical and psychological well-being.

Handling Relationships:

Relationships gives us a sense of belonging and can help us live healthier, happier, and longer lives. They can nurture us through a sense of belonging and sense of purpose. An emotionally intelligent person would be able to handle criticism without denial, blame, excuses, or anxiety.

One of the hallmarks of high emotional intelligence is self-awareness. This means that a person with high EI would be open-minded, good listeners and that they would apologise when they're wrong.

Research proves that people with a lower EI have higher risk of depression or anxiety. That is proportionate to someone understanding their own emotions and that of others, and have trained themselves to respond appropriately, without getting annoyed or angry. Someone with a high EI would know how to lift their own or others spirits up in some complicated situations.

The best part is that EI is a skill that can be learnt at any stage of life. This invaluable skill should be taught in schools as core of the curriculum so that mental health issues can be minimised in children and adults. Until we get there, it's a personal responsibility.

Let's start now, and if not now, when?

SHARON BROWN

**BUSINESS OWNER AT
MO2VATE MEDIA
THE BOOK CHIEF
THE SPEAKERS INDEX**

CHAPTER 28

How to Make Money While You Sleep

By Sharon Brown

A very open statement, YES, but it is possible!

WHY?

The big WHY for me is easy. I want to reduce time spent on screen, reduce stress and on-demand services from clients. I want to spend more time doing other things that I enjoy and not be working 10-hour days. I've done a lot of the hard work already but thankfully have reduced my working hours to Monday to Thursday now.

I had always dreamt about that 'laptop lifestyle' I read about in magazines and thrillers, but I never actually thought that it could be easily attainable.

I started to read the right books, observe the right people and learn that anyone can do this.

Time freedom is the most valuable commodity you can have. If you have time, you have a choice, and if you have a choice, the world is your oyster. That, combined with financial stability and the sky, really is the limit on how you can live your life.

You may think this is outside your capabilities or capacity, but I can tell you first hand you can achieve it, and I'll give you some insight into how in the next section!

HOW?

It's easier than ever to start an online business.

A few years ago, I needed to get my business online as the trend was heading that way, and I believe it will continue down this path.

This means that most potential customers are shopping online for something, whether that be physical goods or digital products or services.

There are three obvious ways to get online:
- Start a membership subscription site
- Offer online courses
- Offer 1-2-1 coaching services online

More and more businesses are heading down this road, with membership sites and online courses popping up everywhere. The key is to do your homework and ask yourself; What service are people looking for?

If you can find a gap in the market anywhere, that's where you should start. Think about your competitors and how they're doing things.

Can you do it better and different?
Is the market already saturated with those businesses or ideas?

Don't copy others; come up with something unique. I know they say no idea is a new idea, but the difference is action, and you can make it unique to you!

You'll have some tasks to do before you can start a business online, and here are the first few to get you going:

- Write down a list of things you are good at and enjoy doing—your strengths and interests.
- Now mark down next to them, which ones set you alight... what are you passionate about?
- Think about services or products you could do around these interests. Are these things that a customer could benefit from? Are they things a customer would want to buy?

- Once you've decided on one, think about creating a simple business plan (1 or 2 pages max)
- You'll need to think about price points, too, so do your due diligence and research what others are charging. Do you want to undercut on price and become a budget brand, or do you want to go middle or high end? Remember, perspectives can associate cheap with little value unless you're targeting a specific low budget audience.

Those are the main points to get you started. Once you've nailed the above, you can start thinking about the intricate details of branding and setting up your website etc.

The laptop lifestyle is not as far away as you think!

CHAPTER 29

Octopus Your Business

By Sharon Brown

There are many ways to scale a business, but one method I find particularly useful and one that I've built my own business on is something I like to refer to as The Octopus Model.

When you have an idea to start a business or you currently have a business your working in, this obviously started with a concept, an idea which you've already put into action. Let's use what some might class as a difficult example to scale...a hairdressing business.

You've trained and then you've opened your salon. You've come a long way from that initial thought and you can see tangible results.

Not only have you started a service business, but you are physically seeing results through your actions.

So how would you expand on a hairdressing business you might ask. It serves its purpose. People book an appointment, they come in, you cut their hair, they leave until the next time. This is all true, but if you have ambition at the heart of you, you might want to think about the next steps!

If I were working in this profession and I'd already opened my own salon, I'd always be looking to expand on it so how would I do it by using the Octopus Method.

Firstly, I'd look at my business as a whole and this is just an example of what I'd be asking, what I'd be answering and what ideas I can implement to move to the next level:

A) **Who do I serve?** My demographic is women between 30 – 45 mainly
   IDEA: Add a discount / new product / new service that will attract an additional demographic for older women
   IDEA: Change your branding to a 'lifestyle look'
B) **Why do I serve them?** To make them feel good about themselves
   IDEA: Host a fashion show or VIP Champagne party
   IDEA: Ask them to fill in a customer satisfaction form to find out what they might like
C) **What do I do for them?** I transform their appearance and build their confidence.
   IDEA: Offer confidence building products and get feedback

IDEA: Hire a 'chair' to a beauty consultant who can do nails within the salon

D) **Where does it happen?** At my salon

IDEA: To attract an older demographic, add a home salon service or a mobile styling service

IDEA: Create an easy online booking service

E) **When do I do this?** Tuesday to Saturday 9am to 5pm

IDEA: Open later two mornings per week and stay open later on those days

IDEA: Hire someone to work the additional days you would normally stay closed

So many opportunities can be built around any business. If you can't see them, ask for help from a business mentor, join a Mastermind Group, hire a reputable coach, learn online, read.

Before too long you will have lots of 'arms' to your business from that original concept and this means lots of access to different income streams. This is where my Octopus Method theory really comes into its own.

TRY IT...you could be building your empire soon and if you would like further help on any of this, do reach out... we have various support initiatives to really help you reach your potential.

CHAPTER 30

Get your Book Published for FREE!

By Sharon Brown

A couple of years ago I never dreamed that I would be a Lead Author in one book never mind a series of them, but that's exactly what has transpired over the past 24 months. It was one of the best decisions I made too and here's why!

As a business owner, first and foremost, this is a fantastic way to give you credibility and to build authority aligned with your business. Your books don't need to be best sellers, just something that aligns with your values and your business. You can gift them to potential clients, you can keep promoting them as another arm to your business and they can be used as lead magnets to build that all important email list.

Why collaborative books you ask? There are many reasons why this is a great way to get started on your writing and publishing journey... see what you think below:

1. You are helping others become published Authors and making their dreams come true – many people may not

know how to go about publishing their own book so you're allowing them the space to become a Co-Author and to work with you first hand.

2. You will be the Lead Author in your books which brings confidence in other books you may want to write – every book you take part in, you can add to your resume either as a Lead Author or Co-Author... it's spreading the word about you and your business and building credibility.

3. As a Lead Author you will set a fee for your Co-Authors to take part which means you won't have to pay for Publishing costs on your own – this can also be profitable and make you an income depending on how many Co-Authors you choose for your book.

4. You are showing people what you're like to work with – this can only be a good thing and it builds confidence in your fellow business owners about your services.

Apart from the above, it allows you to work collaboratively with other people and through that process itself, business relationships are born and can be nurtured.

If you're on the fence and can't imagine yourself becoming a published Author, think again. It's well within your reach and companies like The Book Chief Publishing House specialise in collaborative books to take a lot of the hassle away and to ensure your legal requirements are set up properly.

Something to get you started…

- Think of five different topics you are passionate about and write them down.
- Then list different areas within those topics you could write about. Try and list around 10 bullet points on each topic.
- Now pick the topic you are most passionate about… that's where to start! Each bullet point could be a chapter or a section of your book.

Remember, you only need 24 pages to publish a book on Amazon so aim for that, then work on more!

SUSAN TOTMAN

BUSINESS OWNER AT
VIRTUAL E-SCHOOL
VIRTUAL BIZ CONNECTION

CHAPTER 31

When Disaster Strikes...Will you be Ready?

By Susan Totman

If the last couple of years has taught us anything, it is that life has many unexpected twists and turns. Most of us have experienced many of course, but this threw us into a whole new dimension.

When people typically think of a disaster, what immediately comes to mind is an earthquake, tornado, hurricane, terrorist attack, pandemic or other type of national or worldwide catastrophe. In reality, it can also be something affecting you specifically, such as an abrupt layoff or slack in business, a sudden illness or injury, loss of someone close, family stress, technical failure or many others – the myriad of possible situations is endless.

My experience with personal catastrophes over the 30+ years I've been in business has ranged from major technical failures resulting in loss of client data; illness, and my roof blowing off, rendering not only my home, but my computer equipment and data useless; to the sudden death of my sister in 2017.

Some of my colleagues have had their lives collapse around them without warning. One had her house picked up in a tornado, losing everything. Fortunately, she survived, but lost all of her client data, computer, and files. Another died at a very young age at her desk due to a stroke. Yet another lost everything in a flood.

Preparation for the unknown can be overwhelming – a daunting and uncomfortable task that many of us shy away from as we move about our busy daily lives. We tend to focus on what is in the moment, rather than what 'might' happen, assuming that there is plenty of time.

To use some famous last words, "I'll get around to it." Some people even believe that preparation is bad luck and can trigger or 'jinx' negative events.

Though it may sound harsh, when you're in business serving other people, their priority is not you – it's what you do for them. If you should drop off the grid for any reason without a plan, it leaves them hanging in mid-air, projects unfinished and potentially without access to their data. When push comes to shove, if you aren't able to fulfil the service, their needs are not being met and they will move on. The old adage holds true, "It's not personal, it's business."

As each situation has reared its ugly head, it's had its own unique challenges, forcing me to re-evaluate each time of what worked and what failed as a result of preparation – or lack of it. something as seemingly insignificant as a power outage lasting a few days can wreak havoc in a small business' bottom line.

Large or small, deviations from our normal lives alter our ability to continue as usual if we don't have a plan. Creating even a basic plan helps us to retain some control, delegate if we need to, and reduce the impact to our clients and family.

You can begin with the free disaster plan available on our website.

CHAPTER 32

Collaboration: The Key to a Sustainable Business

By Susan Totman

Throughout the start-up world, you will hear the question, "Who's your competition?" countless times. Pretty much every business planner, marketer, and strategist will ask you that question with good reason. It's a necessary consideration to determine whether your chosen market is a sustainable choice.

Historically, the competition is someone to watch out for. Protect your 'secret sauce' at all costs from the competition so they can't steal your ideas or products. Competition, in many ways, can be good and motivating as it inspires innovation and generates excitement.

We all wanted to be at the top of the class, right? Unfortunately, this mindset also sets us up for a very stressful life as an entrepreneur.

Over the years, it has become apparent to me that pitting myself, my skills and my company against the competition is based on negativity and can cause great stress, anxiety and frustration as we all claw our way to the perceived top of the proverbial mountain, only to realise once there, that the mountain top is just an illusion.

After many years in business following the relatively aggressive competition model, I started to reach out to those I had previously held at arm's length. We discussed where our strengths lie and how we could complement each other. What did we specialise in? what did they specialise in? if we partnered, could we offer more? If we referred to each other based on expertise, could that benefit us all?

Instead of continuing to spend money on advertising that focused on how much better I was than them, I turned it around. I went against all the coaching and strategy advice I've been given my entire adult life about competition, and it WORKS!

Like any business relationship, not every collaboration will work out the way you envision. I have had a lot of successful collaborations, and a few I never want to discuss again, LOL. The important thing is that I didn't give up because one or two didn't work out.

I discovered that focusing on creating business partnerships and collaborative teams instead of how to beat the competition made most of them my friends and colleagues, and much more willing to reach out, offer support or a helping hand. Instead of being wary every time we enter a room – virtual or in person – we are planning new and exciting projects that can benefit all of us.

Similarly, our family business, a bricks and mortar automotive business, got the same results. At first, it's challenging because we human beings are set in our ways. We don't like change, so we tend to baulk or feel like we are not in control. Collaboration does require cooperation and an open mind.

The truth is that YOUR bottom line will improve if you realise that there really is enough work out there for all of us – and we can be better together by creating collaborations that benefit everyone.

TRISH SPRINGSTEEN

BUSINESS OWNER AT PURPLE UNICORN MARKETING ACADEMY

CHAPTER 33

60 Seconds of Insane Courage

By Trish Springsteen

How many times has fear stopped you from grabbing an opportunity to step up and speak, to open your own business, to share your message, your product, service or book?

The answer I'm sure would be too many times. It certainly was for me!

Way back in the Jurassic Period – many, many years ago there was an introvert, a very shy introvert, who was about to embark on her journey into the wide world. If you were to mention to that introvert that she would be a business owner and a speaker, she would have laughed at you.

So how did I get from that shy introvert to where I am today – still an introvert but not so shy, and a business owner. What lessons have I learned on that journey? How did I have the courage to start my own business?

I would never have started my business if not for my greatest lesson. Believing in myself. It took far too long for me to understand and accept who I was. Far too long to realise that I had a message, a story, something of value to share with others.

Once I believed in myself it was empowering. It became the foundation of my having the courage to step up and start a business. Today I celebrate my uniqueness and I accept who I am. In fact, that is part of my business, helping others to own who they are and have the courage to share their uniqueness in their business and with the world.

On my business journey I have learned the value of what I term 60 seconds of insane courage. It's something that has helped me to grow, to grab opportunities and to step outside my comfort zone.

Twenty seconds to acknowledge the negative voices that say, "I can't do that, I'm not good enough, I don't have a message, I can't speak."

Twenty seconds to say STOP and replace the negative with positive, "I am good, I can speak, I do have a message, I can do this."

Twenty seconds to smile, take a deep breath and say YES. Yes, to starting that business. Yes, to stepping up and sharing my message and Yes to grabbing the opportunities that come.

When I look back at my business journey, which started in 2006, I see a journey that has had many ups and downs. The business I have today is different to the business I started.

It has grown and changed according to changes in economy and my personal direction. It has been a journey that has taught me many lessons and one that will continue to teach me lessons.

In these few words I have shared two of my greatest lessons. My question to you is what has your business taught you? Or are you still to start that business because you have let fear stop you?

Believe in yourself, take 60s seconds of insane courage, start now!

BONUS CHAPTERS

By Sharon Brown

SHARON BROWN

**BUSINESS OWNER AT
MO2VATE MEDIA
THE BOOK CHIEF
THE SPEAKERS INDEX**

CHAPTER 34

The Importance of Teamwork in Business

By Sharon Brown

When you make the decision to start your own business, it's a scary prospect for most. You're probably already working a full-time job and have been motivated by one of many things, whether it be money, a dream for the future, a bad experience at work or just knowing you can do it better!

For me, the motivator was rejection. I had been pipped at the post for a promotion that was by all accounts rightfully mine in terms of experience, qualifications, proven results and length of time at the company BUT...as I'm sure many people have experienced, it wasn't to be for one reason or another. That is something I am now very thankful for.

Hindsight is a wonderful thing and looking back it was the kick up the backside I needed! My experience and shift in mindset proved to be a huge motivator which started my journey as a small business owner.

Whatever the motivator or kick start is...do it.

If you can visualise it, then you can do it and you'll never know what could have been, if you don't!

It's a lonely place to start, even though you're surrounded by people who are urging you to go for it. You'll wonder at times, can I really do this and if I can, where will it take me, as there are so many things to think about and learn, and of course, those self-limiting beliefs can creep in at the start.

I thankfully jumped in at the deep end. I had faith in my ability to know what I needed to do at the start and also to realise that I could learn on my feet as I went along. I think Richard Branson's well known quote sums it up, *"If someone offers you an amazing opportunity and you're not sure you can do it, say yes then learn how to do it later."*

My most rewarding learning experience to date was realising the benefits of teamwork in business. Obviously, I'd experienced this in work, but it's different in business and much more supportive if you have the right people around you. For the first couple of years you'll probably be finding your feet and doing things like your business plan and building your website amongst many other things, but my advice would be to build your network from the start. Make those connections with other business owners and build on those relationships as much as possible as those are the people who will become your TEAM.

These work similarly to friendships (and some will become friendships), you'll have different tiers of people, some becoming your closest allies and confidantes, whereas others you know you can ask advice from and they'll happily give it. It's really important to build these relationships and keep them strong.

Help each other and you'll grow your businesses together.

"TOGETHER EVERYONE ACHIEVES MORE" (TEAM)!

If you're a Sole Trader or someone who works on their own, you're probably wondering, how can I have a team when I'm on my own? but it's all a matter of perception! Build your relationships and lean on those people and hopefully they'll lean on you. There is no stronger way to success than to work together and help each other get there. You may get there on your own but it will take you longer so, network, chat to people, take an interest, give a part of yourself and your time and the results will be inevitable.

The most important part of having strong connections to other business owners is the feeling of support you have. No doubt there will be different industries and backgrounds in your network and this is how you get experience by learning from each other. I'm lucky enough to have some great connections with people who have amazing experience in business and life, so I'm confident that I could go to any of them and ask for advice and they would happily give it.

Always try and support the small businesses and use their services and products. Most small businesses who are serious about their business, will really go to work for you and try their best as they have a reputation to build and your money will go a lot further!

CHAPTER 35

7 Top Tips on Creating a Successful Network

By Sharon Brown

The hardest part of any business is trying to engage your audience initially. Getting people to buy your products or services can be, and is, very difficult and probably more so at this point in time, when people are without doubt being more diligent about what they spend their money on.

Be it competition or low attention spans, you'll find the average user gets distracted very easily. I've read that it's gone from 20 minutes 30 years ago, to just 8 seconds nowadays! So...what can you do that may just give you the edge and stop people scrolling past your content for that little bit longer?

Here are a few tips to try that should help you create an engaged network, and which I can honestly say have worked for me in terms of raising awareness, gaining exposure, maintaining interest and most importantly...allowing people to really connect with YOU!

Email everyone you've connected with ASAP after networking, or exchanging business cards or contact details.

This lets potential business partners know how driven and serious you are. You should also always keep in mind that everyone you come across has the potential to end up working with you, so don't dismiss someone just because you don't initially see synergy.

'THE OPPOSITE OF NETWORKING IS NOT WORKING!"

Connect on Social Media!

Do this within 24 hours while you're still fresh in their memory and vice versa. If you can email and connect in the same evening, you'll definitely leave an impression.

Endorse, like, comment or share your new connections posts!

This again brings you to the forefront of their mind. You've now not only connected quickly, but you've shown you're willing to help them look good to their contacts and this will usually let them start to engage with you too!

Arrange to meet for a coffee if your contacts are local!

If you've met business owners through networking, then it's a great opportunity to have that 1-2-1 with them afterwards. This way you'll really get to know about their business and you'll get the opportunity to talk about yours. Look at how you can both potentially help each other either in terms of collaborating or through social media promotion as there is always some way to be supportive to each other.

Make introductions to other contacts – be a connector!

Most businesses work in conjunction with others, whether it be suppliers or consumers, so make introductions to either. You never know who people know that could potentially gain anyone business. You'll be remembered somewhere down the line when you do people favours. Some won't appreciate it of course, but most will, so make it worthwhile and do it without any expectation of gain.

Create a community through a group, meeting or social event!

This is easier than you think but will also take longer than you think. If you're willing to put in the time and effort to really show people the benefits of supporting and promoting each other, they'll eventually see it as you do. This could be in the form of a social media group or an email group where you could invite people to meet up once a month to discuss their businesses etc. There is REAL power in this and once their eyes have been opened, there is no going back!

Don't do a hard sell to your contacts, be honest and ask them if they'd be interested.

People don't like being sold to…however, they don't mind a gentle nudge to let them know you're thinking of them from time to time. Be honest rather than using a bunch of buzzwords which most people can see through…you'll get a lot further with a genuine approach!

That's my top tips for now on creating a network and maintaining your relationship with them! I hope you've found this helpful. These tips are ones which have helped me immensely in building a great network to date…I hope they will for you too.

Just remember the most important thing is COMMUNICATION. Be yourself, be genuine and authentic and take an interest in people and you'll find they'll open up to you too!

CHAPTER 36

How to Deal with Bad Behaviour in Business

By Sharon Brown

Being on the receiving end of bad behaviour from other 'so called' professionals can be a daunting experience. The one thing to remember here is, it's not about you. Just like back in the playground, some people can feel threatened, jealous or insecure of a confident approach.

I've observed the 'pack' behaviour where they will try to break your spirit, the insecure boss who is scared of looking incompetent next to you, and the jealous colleague who will try to win over everyone and exclude you as much as possible!

I've seen it all BUT how do you know the difference between cranky and just plain old unprofessional behaviour? It's true we all have bad days and sometimes we, or others, are on the receiving end of that negativity. It can be a difficult one to work out, but it's important to go with your gut instinct which usually never lets you down.

This is not just down to one gender, or to just lower management desperate to climb the promotional ladder either.

It can also reveal itself at the highest levels of business surprisingly enough.

The question is, what can you do about it? Here are some examples and tips to help you navigate these scenarios if you ever come across them either in your workplace or through your business.

Example – Higher level executive trying to demean you in front of their peers!

It's easy to have an emotive response to this especially if your principles are based on treating everyone with respect. A great way to nip this in the bud straight away is by keeping a stiff upper lip and asking them politely to address any issues with you privately. Do this in front of their peers as it shows you can control your emotions in a tricky situation and lets the perpetrator know you are in control and exercising your emotional intelligence at the highest level. It also shows their peers you are not willing to put up with this sort of behaviour.

As quoted by Dr Steve Maraboli, 'If they do it often, it isn't a mistake; it's just their behaviour."

Example – Being treated differently to others!

For this one it's best to clear the air. It may be miscommunication, it may be a secret resentment that's coming across indirectly, or it may be nothing. Let them know you've noticed it, ask them if there is an issue and if so, the best way to resolve it is to be honest and discuss. If there is an issue, at least you've cleared the air and you can either resolve it properly or move on. If they don't wish to comment then you know you've hit a nerve, as any professional person (who is not holding a grudge) would be mortified they made you feel that way and want to clear the air immediately!

Example – Your boss criticising your work consistently!

You really don't have to put up with this behaviour. Ask them what it is you're doing wrong and what they'd like you to change. If they give clear instruction, implement their wishes. If the criticism continues, then you know it's personal so take action. Tell them you don't appreciate the constant criticism and that it's demotivating. Take them to task for treating you as such. If it doesn't stop then it's an HR issue, and if they do nothing, which in my experience is quite common, then it's time to ask yourself if you really want to continue working in an organisation that allows that behaviour and who clearly doesn't value its employees. Remember though, if you have to ask, then you already know the answer!

Example – Dealing with substance abuse in either your Manager or colleague

This is quite a taboo subject but it does happen! I've experienced two Managers who clearly had an issue with alcohol. After reading up about it, it seems there is not a lot can be done about it (apart from tribunal) unless the company want to take action and admit there is a problem.

My advice for you on this one is GET OUT as soon as you can. You could highlight the issue but there is a very good chance the company already knows there is a problem but is unwilling to deal with it. In my opinion this should be dealt with the same as any illness, as that is exactly what it is. They need help, and by ignoring this, the company are indirectly responsible for the continual decline of that person's health. The affected person will usually be the most plausible and likeable functioning alcoholic whilst they're sober, but as soon as they fall back (which they inevitably will if they don't get help), then you're back on that roller coaster of abuse.

I recognised the second time almost immediately as the same characteristics were displayed as the first time, namely a multitude of excuses as to why they hadn't done something, gone somewhere, or actually turned up on time.

You'll start to be blamed for all their incompetency and most damaging of all…they will lie as much as it takes to save their own skin, no matter how much this might damage your reputation.

If you recognise these signals, then leave anyway as it's not worth hanging around in any circumstances. I stayed for longer than I should have for my own reasons, but it depletes your motivation, confidence and peace of mind so get out fast... and look for a reference elsewhere!

Example – Failure frustration from other professionals

This can come in many shapes and forms but the example I'll use today is another business owner. Their business is not doing well and they are feeling frustrated, angry and scared, so it all comes out on you because you appear to be performing well and doing the right things to get ahead!

You may experience little digs, sarcastic comments, people trying to pick holes in your work, or plain old rudeness, but again you really don't need to put up with this. Their frustrations are THEIR frustrations and shouldn't be directed at you.

Gently ask if they are alright? This shows them you can see a difference in their behaviour. If it continues, ask them why they are taking this out on you? If their tirade persists then you're best taking yourself out of the situation. If they are a close friend, try and offer advice. Some will take it, whilst others will see this again as you having thought about something they should have, and so continue with their grudge fest! It's time to walk away!

Well that's my tips for dealing with some bad behaviour, I hope it's helped someone in some way. In summary, you should never allow people to speak to you disrespectfully or treat you like you're a lesser being than them. It's only a title and company status they have, and remember they can lose that as quickly as it was given to them. Without it, they are no different to anyone else.

CHAPTER 37

5 Reasons Small Businesses need a Website

By Sharon Brown

What is the first thing you do when you see something or hear about something you want to buy? Google it right? When you think about how we as consumers find out pretty much about everything, it's usually a Google search then a skim down the various links which mostly lead us to websites, which we then click on and become one of their unique viewer numbers on their analytics!

If you don't have a website, especially one that looks professional, and you told your potential clients what you do, who you are and what you can do for them, how would they solidify that information in their own mind? Many people are visual and can take information in far more easily if it's in front of them to sift through at their leisure. This is why a professional website (in my opinion) is paramount to any successful business.

I've came across so many small business owners who don't have a website, don't know where to start, and if they do have one, they've attempted it on their own much to their own branding detriment. I did it myself at the start to save money!

Your brand is recognisable. It's the foundation to build your business on and to build authority and credibility. When people continually see that brand, it sticks in their memory. They start associating it with you and what you stand for. Having a logo and website is a sure fire way to start building that brand, and pushing it out there to become a recognisable and reliable ally that sits alongside your principles and personality.

Have a brand strategy before creating either your logo or your website. Be clear from the beginning the kind of image you want to project and ensure your logo and website reflect that vision. Start with your logo, what do you want it to say about you and your business. A good designer should be able to assist you in this.

Here are some reasons you should consider investing in your ideal branding tool:

Gain Credibility

Everyone should know where their customers hang out but on the occasions you don't, how do your prospects reach you? You have to give yourself the best possible chance of creating that opportunity to be found online. A good website gives you instant credibility. It says to your clients that you're serious about what you do and gives them a central point where they can get information on your business and contact you. Clients usually will have a lot of questions, but if the answers are on your website already, it will take the pain out of that initial discovery call.

Amazing Blogs

Billions of people use the internet every day all over the world. If you don't have a footprint on there, where are they going to find you? One of the best ways to do this is a blog on your website with ideal keywords set up for your SEO. Blogs keep your website current and engage new audience members to keep coming back and signing up.

Social Media

Once you've created your amazing content, you can share on your social media platforms with a link back to your website. This not only increases your website visitors, it could gain you a new audience on social media. Make sure you have your social links on your website too which will allow your viewers to share on their own platforms.

Share your News

You can post so many things on your website i.e., blogs, press releases, events, reviews, publications and much more, and these can all help you climb up the search rankings. You have an instant hub where visitors can learn everything they need to know about your business and what you have planned, and this creates a relationship between you and your prospects or visitors.

Create a Database

Adhere to GDPR rules always and don't 'cold' email someone. Build your database of genuinely interested parties and gather the information through your website. This is a great hub to collect data on your subscribers and customers and create a valuable database. Whether you're creating freebies for visitors to sign up, or a forum where you can welcome visitors to take part in debates or post material, it's a great way to bring people together.

Having an attractive and well-designed website for your business creates an opportunity to influence your potential prospects' mindset and helps you to generate more sales.

There are many more reasons having a website is good for you and your brand (if done correctly). It also doesn't have to cost you a fortune if you shop around.

There are other costs to consider too i.e. domain and hosting etc, but all can be done at a very affordable cost.

CHAPTER 38

9 Content Marketing Facts You Need to Know!

By Sharon Brown

Did you know that headline content makes up 50% of your article or blog post effectiveness? Or that headlines with numbers generate on average 73% more social shares and engagement? According to the *Content Marketing Institute* this is indeed the case!

This subject has always fascinated me, and it is the basic psychology of marketing at play here, but if done correctly the results are mind blowing. In a specific post on LinkedIn, I reached nearly 200,000 views just by asking a simple question that clearly resonated with the audience. Here are a few statistics taken from various sources to help you on the road to a 'Viral Post'.

Odd numbers work better

The brain believes odd numbers more than even numbers, and apparently they help people recall information more easily. You can increase your click through rates by up to 20% if you use these in your headline according to the *Content Marketing Institute.*

Blogging is best!

The top three content marketing tactics are Blogging, Social Media and Case Studies, with Blogging coming out on top at 65% *(excerpt from LinkedIn Technology Marketing Community).*

Everyone needs a content marketing strategy

Content marketing will help you prepare and plan for reliable and cost-effective sources of website traffic and new leads.

Your time matters

81% of marketers found that increased traffic occurred with as little as 6 hours per week invested in social media marketing *(Social Media Examiner)*

We're spending less

Content marketing costs 62% less than traditional marketing and generates about 3 times as many leads *(DemandMetric)*

Content needs to be relevant

65% of B2B marketers struggle to define what content is effective and what isn't *(Content Marketing Institute)*

Database essentials

B2B buyers are most likely to share their name and email address in exchange for Webinars, White Papers, Analyst Reports and eBooks *(DemandGen)*. Turn your blog posts into an eBook and try to collect as much information on your subscribers as possible before the conversion rates drop off.

Biggest challenge

60% of B2B content marketers say producing engaging content is their biggest challenge *(Content Marketing Institute / Marketing Profs)*

Build your customer portfolio

78% of customers believe that organisations providing custom content are interested in building good relationships *(Key Difference Media)*.

So, in summary, we all need to be spending more time on creating content that really engages our audiences and brings value. The Pareto Principle is one that really stands the test of time and highlights that 80% of the effects come from 20% of the causes and this should also be applied to your content management.

CHAPTER 39

Reliability = Credibility

By Sharon Brown

Reliability is the key to trust, loyalty, integrity, and ultimately credibility. If you give your word to someone, then that should be your bond. We are all human of course and life does sometimes throw us a curveball, but even if you have to go back on your word because of circumstances beyond your control, let people know!

Forgetting to do something can be commonplace at certain times in life, but if you fall foul to this, make a heartfelt apology and be honest about it with the person. If you're running late or can't make something, then let the person know beforehand if it's within your power to do so. Most people never purposely forget or let people down.

The other skill involved here is communication, which is the foundation of everything. If you can't, or don't, communicate, things get lost or don't get done, or worse, get done wrongly. As is said by Paul Carrick Brunson, "Call when you say you will. Show up when you say you will. Inconsistency destroys trust and trust is the foundation of all relationships."

You will have many instances where other business owners will prove unreliable, and not because of life circumstances, but purely because they just don't value your time or effort to turn up. You'll hear some unbelievable excuses and sometimes no excuse at all, and sometimes you may need to point out that they were late, didn't call, stood you up at a meeting etc.

The question you should be asking yourself if this happens is, would YOU do business with someone who let you down with no apology or acknowledgement of their tardiness?

If red flags show themselves with other business owners, do listen to your gut. Once may be a mistake but if it's continued behaviour and lack of work ethic, they are probably not going to be a good fit around you.

The same can happen with lack of communication which is commonplace. Again, things outside of their control can happen, or sometimes they may just be overwhelmed with too much work...do allow for this human part of life as it's something we can all go through at times. The main point is about honesty and integrity and explaining to the other person. If you forgot, say you forgot, don't make up excuses for the sake of it.

Looking credible in business is so important and this usually comes through word of mouth and testimonials so BE RELIABLE...It's so underrated and yet extremely valued.

CHAPTER 40

The Importance of Celebrating Your Wins

By Sharon Brown

How often do you write down your achievements, regardless of how big or small they may be?

You may think they're NOT worth taking note of because they haven't made a massive impact, but you shouldn't forget that every small step adds up!

We never recognise just how far we're moving ahead at times, and the little goals that are taking us towards our bigger goals each week, month and year, so it's important to note these down and 'pat yourself on the back', even if you feel it's not much. Every little bit counts and your larger goals are all made up of many small steps. It doesn't matter if it's personal or professional...if it has made you feel good, then it all counts!

A great exercise I do is to write down my achievements on post it notes, fold them up and pop them in a jar. The aim of this is to save them until the end of the year where I can have an 'opening' celebration just before Christmas. Can you imagine the sense of pride doing this just before the New Year comes in?

It's even better doing this with colleagues and getting together to open them together and celebrate everyone's achievements.

Whatever you choose to do, do try and take a note of all your small wins during the course of each month. You will be amazed at how many you have, and make sure to share these with others too. It will keep up the momentum!

If you can match these wins against any business strategy or plan you may have, you may feel even more elation at the end of the year.

Many small business owners give up within the first three years of trading, because they feel the struggle of getting new clients, growing their business, tech issues, demotivation, lack of work ethic and many more reasons.

Listing your small wins can provide much needed self-motivation and focus, which can be hard in the early days. A great way of doing this is by downloading a mini business plan which sets your goals for the year and allows you to strategise how you're going to reach them. It's a worthwhile exercise.

CHAPTER 41

How to Succeed at Collaboration

By Sharon Brown

I'm a massive fan of collaboration, so much so that I built my very first online platform around the ethos 'collaboration over competition'. What I'd like to get across in this article really is, YES do collaborate and do look for people that will share your vision, BUT choose your collaborative partners wisely. I always like to give people the benefit of the doubt and take someone on face value. My failing at times though is I don't listen to those little nagging doubts that are trying to push me in the right direction. Because I want to believe and because I know my own values, I push them aside in favour of the other chatter, 'I'm just being paranoid', or 'I'm over analysing', or the worst one, 'my expectations are too high'.

I know every single one of us has these at any given time about certain people. It's built into us, and I would say especially women who are naturally intuitive. Don't ignore these thoughts and feelings. I've ignored them all too often in the past because I want to believe everyone is equal and is kind and has integrity...THEY DON'T!

I would never get into a legal partnership and start a company again with someone. That was a lesson learned many years ago. A collaboration should still be contracted, but it's not quite as damning as starting an actual registered company with someone and partnering up.

Think about your values. What is important to you? For me, I hold integrity, honesty, loyalty, and trust at the very top of my list.

Here are some DO's and DON'Ts to think about before you go into business or collaborations with anyone. These are observations I've made over the years and are meant as a guide…

- DON'T jump in feet first because it sounds exciting

- DON'T give up your own ideas to align with someone else

- DON'T give away all your business smarts on the first stretch

- DON'T plough money into fancy websites, marketing and advertising until you do some market research

- DON'T just trust someone's word that they're honest and have no agenda…witness it for yourself

- DO get to know someone first, what their values are and the way they work

- DO communicate regularly to ensure you both have your vision aligned

- DO be cautious, and if you get those nagging doubts, listen to them

- DO observe your partner's habits…are they winging it? Are they riding your coat tails? Are they connecting with all of your connections? Some people do have an agenda other than your project!

- DO watch the language they are using when talking about your project…you'll know how you feel when you see it. Is it inclusive? Are they taking credit for everything or things which they shouldn't be taking credit for?

Take note of body language, writing form and peoples responses to certain things, this will help you pick up on any red flags.

Collaboration is the one way that your business will thrive more quickly and wider, IF you choose the right people.

If you are thinking about collaborating, do consider the points above as guidelines only. We all have our own experiences, but I hope this will help you make the right decision.

CHAPTER 42

How 50+ Women Are the New Superpower

By Sharon Brown

Have you noticed the change?

There seems to be a big shift in 50+ women starting businesses and taking ownership of their lives. It's everywhere, new women influencers are emerging and more women than ever are taking control of their own destiny. Business and health seem to be at the forefront of this new what I would call 'superpower' but maybe that's because I'm in this bracket myself.

When I look back to my 20's and 30's, it feels like someone else's story. I didn't have the right head for business or health, or probably relationships for that matter, and I never thought for one minute I'd be where I am now, married, laptop lifestyle, business owner and entrepreneur, mentor, and mother to two beautiful 'fur babies'

I've always been confident about my abilities, although I didn't really value them, or myself in my younger days. I didn't feel worthy of having a 'leader' position and always applied for less than I was capable of. When I hit my forties, things started to become clearer, they started to change in every way. I realised those I was working for had no vision or ability to empower others, and were happy sticking with the status quo. What a stifling environment it is when you are confined by others lack of innovation or creativity.

Those of us who are in our 50s and beyond, heading towards the dreaded menopause, or been there and done it, I'm sure will agree, something changes in us. You care less about what others think and you feel far more comfortable in your own skin. Ego takes a back seat and impressing others is the last thing on your mind. Your tolerance levels go down and you find it easier to remove toxic people from your life.

It's not all plain sailing of course and some of the other things I've noticed are changes to my physical appearance, more ailments, eyesight is worse, you gain weight more easily and lots of other little irritations, but the positives far outweigh the negatives!

Some things which I've realised and maybe you can relate to too, if you're in this middle zone of life like me:

- Being over 50 feels like the start of something exciting.

- You know you are a strong woman but also not as invincible as you or everyone else thought you were.

- Your self-respect means far more now than ever before.

- You recognise that you're unique and your abilities far outweigh what value others have put on you in the past.

- You are confident about speaking up and speaking out, you have an opinion and you're not scared to share it.

- You recognise that not everyone will like your views or the way you work, but you're happy with yourself and the need not to change these views to suit others.

- You value respect, loyalty and honesty more than anything and those who share these values will become your inner tribe.

- You are comfortable releasing those who don't bring you peace of mind or joy.

- You can spot the manipulators or narcissists instantly and you don't feel the need to argue back with them or bow to emotional blackmail.

- You recognise those with an agenda and the people pleasers who would sell you out to save their own skins.

- You understand that those who talk behind your back are trying to win allies but this is down to their own insecurities and lack of self-worth.

- You know that your HEALTH is, and will now be, your number one priority and should never be taken for granted.

- Everyone who talks about taking time out for self-care has actually been through a hard time and is trying to save you from going through it too.

- Taking time out and pampering your soul is one of the best things you can do.

- Time with others who share your views and values is something you yearn for.

- You realise that time with your parents is limited and they'll never be replaced.

These are just some of the things I've become very aware of in the past few years, I hope you can relate to it too.

EPILOGUE

Thank you for purchasing a copy of this book.

As a Small Business Owner, we hope you have found this book insightful, whether you are starting out on your journey or you've been doing it for many years, there is still learning in this book.

The Authors have reflected on their own experiences and things they have learned along the way in order to help you, the reader, forge your path in the right direction and to learn by their mistakes.

The Authors are spread across various continents and have shared what they think you will find useful in your self-employment journey.

If you would like to share your own knowledge or insight, please do submit your business article to us at mo2vatemagazine.com up until 18th November. The website will change to mo2vatemedia.com after this date, allowing you to submit on either one.

Preview of "GUIDE TO A HEALTHIER LIFESTYLE" (Volume One)

"Specific Adaptions" by Martin Sharp

"Have you ever noticed how each athletes body shape changes depending on the sport they are playing?

Perhaps when watching athletes, you can see the sizeable muscular wedge shape in the great rugby players with wide broad shoulders, muscular arms and legs with narrow hips? Compared to Olympic swimmers who often have long slender bodies, with long arms providing a wider reach and are potentially more flexible and nimbler. Yet have you ever wondered what that difference in body shapes actually means to you?"

Preview of "STORIES FROM AROUND THE GLOBE" (Volume One)

"Guardian Angels and Knitting a Life" by Andrea Hochgatterer

"Ouch, my ear, get off! I try and swat the pain away like an annoying fly. "She is coming round! Hello love, you are safe, and I am her to look after you, can you hear me? Can you open your eyes?

I am trying to make sense of what is happening, my eyes are straining to focus. I can hear a lot of commotion around me, there are blurred noises and faces, I move to get up.

ABOUT THE BOOK CREATOR

SHARON BROWN moved to the West Midlands in 2003 from Glasgow in Scotland. After a wide-ranging career in Event Management, Marketing, Project Management and board level support in various industries, Sharon started an Events Agency in 2015 which has grown into Lydian Group Ltd.

After realising that business was heading more towards the online digital space, Sharon launched four online platforms, the first being a Women in Business platform in 2018 with a mission of creating 'Collaboration over Competition'. Two further projects were launched during lockdown with the aim of helping small business owners build their brands through speaking, writing, publishing, and collaborative working. MO2VATE Magazine was born in 6 weeks from concept to implementation and received a fantastic following through its subscribers and supporters. It's now seeing a complete facelift this year ready for its relaunch as MO2VATE Media, seeing it evolve as a membership driven business and information hub.

The Speakers Index was the third platform to be launched as Sharon saw a gap in the market around Speaking Agencies and the lack of promotion towards their speakers. The Speakers Index is an online directory which also houses a quality Speakers Magazine highlighting the speakers' talents. Members are encouraged to create a full profile giving all the information needed by an Organiser who can then contact them directly through their contact details on the website or in the magazine.

The Book Chief Publishing House is Sharon's latest project, launched in 2021, already with an impressive resume of clients and Authors. Sharon's vision was to provide an all-in-one affordable publishing service turning small business owners into credible authors through a robust and structured process. The Book Chief portfolio has exponentially grown during 2022 and continues to build huge momentum.

SERVICES

MO2VATE MEDIA

MO2VATE is a global digital business hub covering topics across business industries, health, inspiration, lifestyle, politics, opinion/research based information, entrepreneur insights and many other topics, founded by Sharon Brown.

Formerly known as MO2VATE Magazine, this new platform launches in November 2022 with a completely new concept to share important information globally.

All articles are written by business owners and the project is managed by independent entrepreneurs. The online hub runs yearly International Awards and produces various books written by the Contributors who are part of the MO2VATE community.

Mo2vatemedia.com
editor@mo2vatemagazine.com

THE BOOK CHIEF PUBLISHING HOUSE

The Book Chief Publishing House was born during the latter end of the pandemic with a mission to support business owners on their path to becoming credible Authors.

The Book Chief publishes every genre, type and size of book and advises on every step of producing your book from book covers, titles, book descriptions, your best chance to become a best-selling Author and much more.

The Book Chief has a great track record in customer service and of producing great results for your book both in layout, editing, design and marketing.

As a one-stop shop for all your Publishing needs, and payment plans to spread the cost, it should be the first stop for those looking to publish and spread the word about their book!

Thebookchief.com

sharon@thebookchief.com

THE SPEAKERS INDEX

The Speakers Index is an online directory for speakers and event organisers designed to improve their chances of being seen by the right people.

We produce a quarterly magazine where each speaker features on a double page spread. The magazine is sent out through social media and to our email list on each publication.

Working similar to an agency but without any additional fees or commission, The Speakers Index also creates events to allow speakers to participate and be seen.

Thespeakersindex.com

sharon@thespeakersindex.com

Printed in Great Britain
by Amazon

87879672R00112